Industry 5.0 = Industry 4.0 + Society 5.0

"Technology for People"

With real case examples and scenarios
from service industries
(Hospitals, Hospitality, Recreation & Education)

Mune MOĞOL SEVER (PhD)

Technology for People

© LITERATÜRK academia 339
İnceleme-Araştırma 317

Ağustos 2021

Yayınevi Editörleri: **Salih TİRYAKİ – Emre Vadi BALCI**
Genel Yayın Yönetmeni: **İsmail ÇALIŞKAN**

ISBN 978-625-7606-19-6

T.C.
Kültür ve Turizm Bakanlığı
Yayıncı Sertifika No: **16195**

Kapak Tasarım: DIZGIMIZANPAJ.com
Baskı Öncesi Hazırlık: **Mehmet ATEŞ**
meh_ates@hotmail.com

Baskı & Cilt: **Bulut Dijital Matbaa San. Tic. Ltd. Şti.**
Musalla Bağları Mh. İnciköy Sk. No. 1/A   Selçuklu/KONYA
KTB S. No: **48120 -** Basım Tarihi: **AĞUSTOS 2021**

KÜTÜPHANE BİLGİ KARTI
- Cataloging in Publication Data (CIP) -

MOĞOL SEVER, Mune
Technology for People

ANAHTAR KAVRAMLAR
Endüstri 5.0, Endüstri 4.0, Toplum 5.0, Dijital Dönüşüm, Hizmet İşletmeleri
Keywords
Keywords –Industry 5.0, Industry 4.0, Society 5.0, Digital Transformation, Service Industries

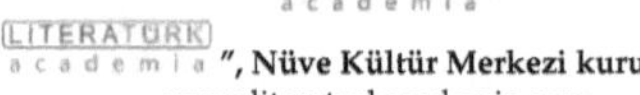

" academia ", **Nüve Kültür Merkezi kuruluşudur.**
www.literaturkacademia.com

/ Nkmliteraturk

M. Muzaffer Cad. Rampalı Çarşı Alt Kat No: 35-36-41
Meram / KONYA Tel: 0.332.352 23 03 Fax: 0.332.342 42 96

Ул. М. Музаффер, рынок Рампалы, нижний этаж № 35-36-41
Мерам, КОНЬЯ, тел.: +90 332 352 23 03,
факс: +90 332 342 42 96

Dağıtım: **EMEK KİTAP**
Akçaburgaz Mah. 3137. Sk. Ali Rıza Güvener İş Merkezi No: 28
Esenyurt / İSTANBUL
www.emekkitap.com - Telefaks +90 212 671 68 10
Дистрибьютор: **EMEK KITAP**
Район Акчабургаз, ул. Али Рыза 3137, бизнес центр «Гювенер» № 28,
Эсеньюрт / СТАМБУЛ
www.emekkitap.com – Телефакс: +90 212 671 68 10

ORTA ASYA OFFICE:
Mikrareyon Kok Jar/23   Bishkek / KYRGYSZTAN
Tel: +996 700 13 50 00   -   Telefaks: + 996 552 13 50 00
ОФИС В ЦЕНТРАЛЬНОЙ АЗИИ:
Микрорайон Кок Жар/23   Бишкек / КЫРГЫЗСТАН
Тел.: +996 700 13 50 00 – Телефакс: +996 552 13 50 00

Industry 5.0 = Industry 4.0 + Society 5.0

"Technology for People"

With real case examples and scenarios
from service industries
(Hospitals, Hospitality, Recreation, Education)

Mune MOĞOL SEVER (PhD)

Mune MOĞOL SEVER (PhD)

The author was born in Savur/MARDİN. She has double major in industrial engineering and economics. After she has worked as a production engineer in several manufacturing industries she started to work in Anadolu University in 2007 as a Research Assistant. She has completed her MA in 2009 and PhD in 2015 in Anadolu University. She is giving following courses: Operations Management in Tourism Management, Quality Management in Service Industries, Quality Management, Ergonomics in the same university.

To My Family

ACKNOWLEDGMENT

I would like to express my biggest and sincere appreciation to my husband and colleague Prof. Dr. Necip Serdar Sever for his help and encouragements throughout this book. I will give my hugs and kisses and thanks to my twins: My Daughter İlayda İlkim and to My Son Oğuzkaan for relieving my stress and helping me relaxing with their charm. I am obliged to acknowledge my appreciations to my father Mehmet Moğol and to my mother Ferah Zekiye Moğol; they are the reason of my existence and for their unconditional support. Other thanks to my sisters Dr. Merve Moğol (MD.) Müge Moğol (MA) for their support and their sister ship.

APERTIO

This book aims to explain main components and technologies of Industry 5.0 (I 5.0). It is also called Society 5.0 (S 5.0) and first introduced in Japan. The I 5.0 is originated from I4.0. The main idea behind I50 is to reach Man_Machine (M/C)-Robot collaboration by using I4.0 technologies. I5.0 is not a threat for human existence; on the contrary, it is for the benefit of human being.

The days of pandemic, which we are living in, shows to enterprises that to accelerate in digitalization is become more important and must be urgently implemented than ever before. Online education, online shopping, online MD appointment etc. emerges and suddenly become a part of our normal life. People manage and monitor their business ventures at home without going the facility via Apps, or online communication Technologies. By the help of 3D and other devices, DIY (Do It Yourself) activities were increased more than ever. This rather unusual situation may become a routine behavior of our lives.

I 5.0 is a philosophy for integration of elders to new technologies via robots (collaborative robots-CoBots), artificial intelligence and many others means. I5.0, emerge as a new revolution after I4.0. The main technologies are same as I4.0 but in new revolution, it is planned to focus on to enhance adaptation of whole society with those technologies and create an ecosystem for people to work together with technologies. That is why scholars call this philosophy as a new revolution as I5.0 (Nahavandi, 2019; Longo et al., 2020; Ozkeser, 2018). Throughout the book terms I5.0 and S5.0. Interchangeably.

Technological background of I5.0 is as same as I4.0 but more advanced and much faster. Some of these technologies of I5.0 are internet of everything, Cyber Physical System, 5G, CoBots and artificial intelligence. Since it is aimed to provide human-machine integration, collaborative robots and artificial intelligence are mostly used in I5.0 revolution. In addition, 5G technologies makes internet available in everywhere and for everyone.

The Bio economy has become an important subject in Industry I5.0. Comparing with past revolution however, using same technologies in I.4.0, with S5.0 revolution enterprises are forced to continue their operations with using renewable energy resources. In doing so, they will contribute to protect environment. While operating in a high speed and low cost conditions they are also faced with taking on responsibility for sustainability. Especially in block chain with the help of smart contract, the all parties in chain can verify the the origin of main components of the finished product in each process. Since the whole process are visible for all parties they can controlled the materials as if they are natural and renewable. In addition, they be informed about the process of using energy in operations and energy harvesting methods, amount of water used in production phase etc. The business enterprises are virtually mandated by consumers as well as market climate to pursue business practices that are not detrimental to environment. Thus, businesses are dictated by the market conditions and by the consumers that they apply ecological production methods in their processes.

In this new revolution, it is aimed to create human-machine integrated and digitalized ecosystem. In this ecosystem data sharing and management is managed digitally from supplier to the end user (end to end) will be possible make nearly simultaneous and by each users in the ecosystem.

Eventually, during the days of pandemic, virtually all works and processes will be done from a distance without going to the facility. There is also one point has to be mentioned some are believe the next revolution, Industry 6.0 (I 6.0) will make it more distant by managing the whole processes via Apps.

In this book, I5.0 and its technologies will be explained and some of the cases from manufacturing and service industries will be outlined. Last section of this book is a scenario-based approach for service industries in their major physical contact point.

Dr. Mune MOĞOL SEVER

CONTENTS

TABLES LISTS

FIGURES LISTS

FROM INDUSTRY 1.0 TO I 5.0

A SHORT VIEW TO INDUSTRIAL REVOLUTIONS (I 1.0 to I 5.0)

When we look at chronological development to industrial revolutions, we see the mechanical period as the *first industrial revolution (I 1.0).*

In 1780, the steam-powered engines were started to be used in manufacturing. By that way the processes were done more quickly and efficiently and thus, the less amount of labor were needed in manufacturing processes.

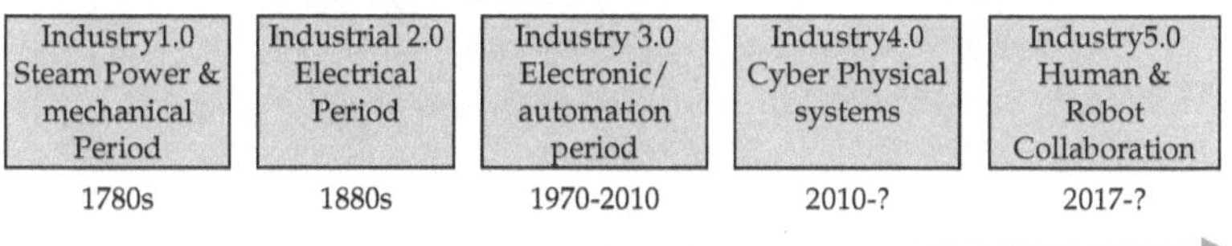

Figure 1. From I 1.0 to I 5.0

After the midst of 1880, the more strong and durable materials such as steel were began to use in machine producing instead of iron. In addition, steam power displaced with electrical power in manufacturing. By using electrical power the speed of production and amount of products were increased significantly. In this period, the World population were increased and meet demand of population the *I 2.0 Mass Production* term has begun.

Henry Ford and its Model T cars were the main milestone in I2.0. Ford has created and used production line system in the manufacturing area. By production line logic the raw materials enter from the point and the finished product were appeared at the end of production line. By this system, the speed of production and the amount of product was increased systematically. In addition, human intervention is decreased with using production line manufacturing system.

Figure 2. I 2.0 Mass Production and Ford' Model T Car
https://www.allaboutlean.com/flow-shop/henry-ford-model-t-1921/,
(09.08.2020).

The division of labor and so many management theories were emerged with working in production line system. Coming years, in addition to electrical devices electronic devices were appeared. Since therefore the next revolution, become *Industry 3.0 (I3.0)* electronic/Automation period.

Figure 3. Third Industrial revolution and robot arms in manufacturing
Resource: https://www.atlanticcouncil.org/blogs/futuresource/an-emerging-third-industrial-revolution/,(Wikimedia) (09.08.2020).

Next revolution called *Industry 4.0*. Industry 4.0 (I 4.0) is a strategic initiative of the German government that was adopted as part of the "High-Tech Strategy 2020 Action Plan" in 2011 (Lydon, 2014).

In this production period, the whole objects in the value chain such as: products, semi-products, machines (M/C), robots etc. has given an IP address. By this way, the real-time communication with objects in the production system is possible (Posada et al., 2015).

The main reasons of industrial revolutions can be named as: (TÜSİAD, 2016):

- The social interaction and as called regional interaction waves between countries

- The rising new economies and globalization

- The technologic developments and trends such as possibility to reach internet and development of platform Technologies.

- The scarcity of resources and globally increasingly Meta movement such as environmental and security fears.

I4.0 has created new business model, enterprises management, customer and new product mentality. In this understanding, from end-to-end network, such as from supplier to the end user, has developed and each object in the system managing itself and has become a smart objects (Shafiq, Sanin, Toro & Szczerbicki, 2015.) Accordingly, customers let us say prosumer, can intervene the processes from beginning, maybe starting designing phase, and they will shape the product as they want. Thus, enterprises has to change completely the processes (Qin, Liu & Grosvenor, 2016). Customers, let us say prosumer, can create a very new and complicated product that is planned in the beginning of the processes.

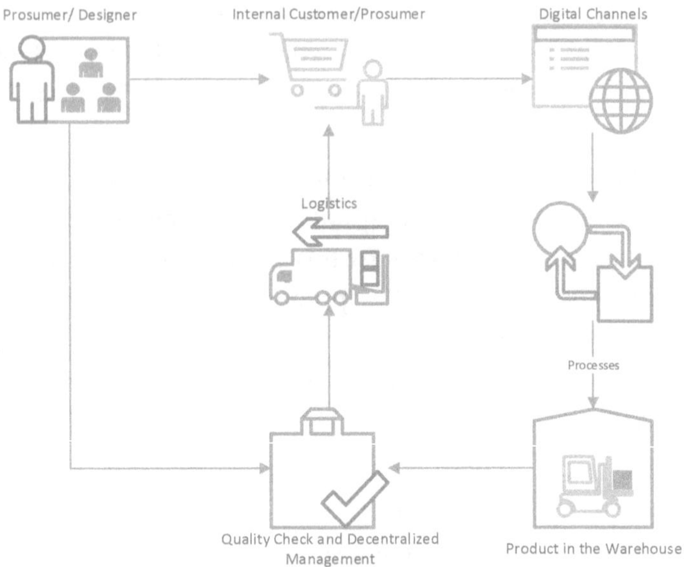

Figure 4. I 4.0 general framework in the operations

With I 4.0, there comes decentralized management, instantaneous control will be possible in each stage, human intervention will be decreased. By this way, the percentage of error and amount of scrap will be minimized and productivity and efficiency will increase. Since the organizational structure is horizontal making decisions, will more quick (simultaneous) than before. In addition to those since controlling and monitoring the processes in each stage simultaneously, the managerial approach will be more transparent and objective than before. The enterprises has to follow these rules with this so-called new generation production approach comes with I4.0:

- To increase the quality of production
- To producing more productive
- Decrease the cost of production by following the rules for environmental protection and sustainability requirement.

Eventually, Industry 5.0 is a Revolution! It is known and called as Society 5.0 I5.0, aims to provide an ecosystem that man and machines work together in a harmony. The philosophy behind I5.0 is to create solutions to facilitate life by help of using robots or machines, which can interact with human via cyber physical system and artificial intelligence. By means of machines, objects and man can interact with each other. Since everyone and everything become smart, the goal of being smart society, which is the motto of S5.0, can be reached. It is why this new revolution is called as S 5.0: super smart society.

Since I5.0 is new, a paradigm there are not so many studies has seen done in so far. On top of this, in practice it is confused with I4.0. Therefore, it is important to point of differences between them. In Table1 differences between I4.0 and I5.0 is pointed based on selected criteria.

Table 1. *The Differences between I 4.0 and I 5.0*

CRITERIA	I 4.0	I 5.0
Aims	Technology without human	Technology for human and working with human
Environmental Responsiveness	• Renewable energy resources • Electric power • Fossil fuel	• Renewable energy resources
Digital environment	Cyber Physical Systems (CPSs)	CPSs+Robots+Artifical Intelligence
Production approach	Mass customization	Mass personalization
Data usage	Digital data usage	Smart data usage
Human_M/C Interaction	Coordination between M/Cs and information systems	Collaboration and adaption between man-M/C
Style of doing job	Decreasing processing time and costs	Decreasing processing time and costs by means of working precisely and creatively
Aims of digitization	Digitization and automation	With using advanced technologies globalize of production systems
Internet	Internet of things	Internet of everything, everyone and everywhere
Speed	With a high speed	Using 5Gs

Compiled from Javaid & Haleem, 2020

As it is emerged in 2016 in Japan, S5.0 (I 5.0) is aimed to provide sustainable development with human focused Technologies (Shiroishi et al., 2019). The main idea behind S5.0 philosophy is to avoid giving repetitive task to human. Doing this, people will have more time for themselves and quality of their life will be increased with delegating tasks monitors to robots and Machines (M/Cs).

I5.0 is the generic name for transforming to super smart society. With I5.0 not only production and service systems but also monetarily, financial and technological transformation will come true. In this new paradigm, to adapt enterprises can do following:

- Make production more quickly and accurately
- Communicate with supplier simultaneously
- Conduct research and development(R&D) with feedback or help of customers who are in every stage of production
- Make transfer any financial assets in a just seconds (block chain technologies and cryptocurrencies)
- Manage its own portfolio
- Print its raw materials with 3B, 4B, 5B printers

In addition, people can:

- Create print prepare its meals (robots, printers)
- Delegate his/her tasks to robots
- Not used physical wallet because of digital money.

In E5 era where custom-tailored manufacturing is, widespread has some aspects of which makes life more easily. One of them is new type of printers. With this new printer technology, it is possible to print more accurate and smooth surfaces and no need to make any extra work on finished product. With these printers, it is possible to make models and manufacture complicated product precisely as planned and by using very little raw materials. Also in this new production approach, it is suggested that firms should use much more renewable materials. This type of production can help making manufacturing more efficient and help companies to reduce amount of waste.

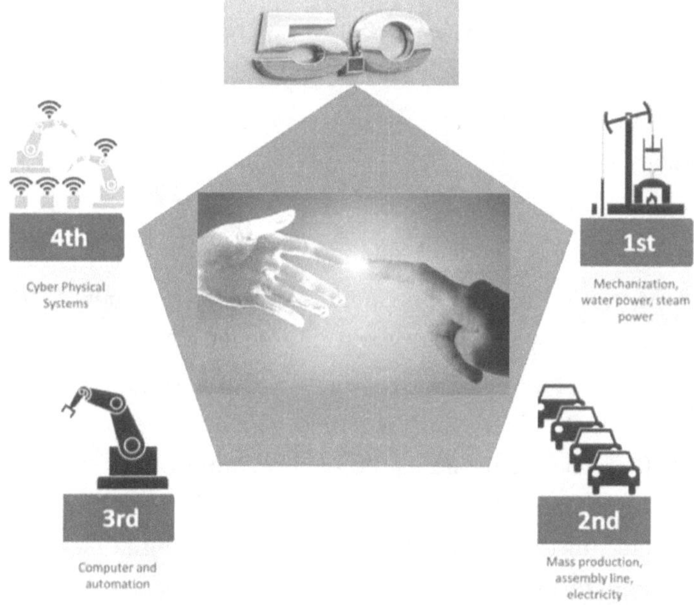

Figure 5. Industrial Revolutions

Rada (2020)

With I5.0, revolution creativity of human, speed, and accuracy of robots come together and collaboration will be increased. In doing so productivity will be increased (European Economic and Social Committee, 2020).

Addition to Technologies of I4.0 in I5.0:

- Using of artificial intelligence will increase
- Collaborative robots will be more common

- Technology and human interaction and collaboration will increase
- Producing personalized product is more possible and will become faster
- Awareness of sustainable production will increase
- Use of renewable resources will increase
- Cyber security has become important subject.

Comparing with I4.0, I 5.0 especially focuses on three themes:

- Man-robots collaborations
- More use of artificial intelligence
- More sustainable production ecosystem (renewable energy resources, healthy and safe food etc.

The first step of transformation in I5.0 is digitization of all the components in system like; objects, man, machines. In reality, I5.0 can be identified as the next revolution after digitalization. The digitalization process started mainly in I4.0 should be completed in this period Enterprises should digitalized whole the system form end to end.

INDUSTRY 5.0

1. INDUSTRY 5.0 AND RELATED TERMS

In this part of the book subjects related with I5.0 such as digital transformation, cybernetics and self-regulating systems will be discussed.

1.1. Digital Transformation

Digitalization at the work place refers to the integration of digital technology in routine work. By this, way data convert to digital form (Shamim et al., 2017).

Digitalization is connecting society, sectors, and means in order for collecting, analyzing and making an action after analyzing digital data (Wirtschaft, 2015).

Increasing in mobile technologies, widespread use of internet and 5G, smart devices and sensor technologies boosting digital transformation. In same manner mineralization in computer and electronic devices and possibility to integrate and embed them to other devices easily, increase the percentage of personalization (Beigl & Gellersen, 2003).

The main subjects that enterprises focuses on is setup and operating cost of establishing I5.0 technologies. Digitalization means costs for enterprises by means of investing sensors cyber physical systems, software's, machines, robots etc. in the beginning they are faced with setup costs after start up there is also operating costs will be added.

Although managers believed that operating setup and running costs are high for I5.0, while thinking agility and flexibility of production, getting rid of lighting, heating and insurance cost and doing jobs with less person it can be said that overall costs will be less than before. Even costs of Enterprise Resource Planning (ERP) and Manufacturing Executive Systems (MES) set up and running costs are much higher (Moeuf, Pellerin, Lamouri, Giraldo Barbaray, 2018). In addition, the logic of operating with less raw material in I5.0 by means of additive manufacturing is also decrease the material costs (Oettmeier & Hofmann, 2017). It is directly affect the general costs positively.

The differences between enterprises accept the principles of I5.0 and not accepted ones are given in Table 2.

Table 2. Enterprises adapted I5.0 vs. traditional enterprises

COST ITEMS	THE ENTERPRISE ADAPTED I5.0 TO ITS PROCESSES	TRADITIONAL ENTERPRISE
Software	Investing to the software	The cost of setup, reporting and maintained of ERP, MES etc. systems
Reporting	In means of M/C, deep learning algorithm the latent pattern of data will analyzed and reports simultaneously	Data analysis will done by system analyst not simultaneously
Maintenance	Autonomously done and system will not stop	Not autonomously done and system can be stops for a while
Decision making	Autonomously done by system	Decision maker will do/control the process
Error	Depends on reliability of robots (very low)	Depending on the decision maker (in most of the cases high depending on the # and experience of decision makers)
Productivity	Since inputs are controlled by the system, productivity is high	Since the man-M/C interaction is low, the productivity is high respectively
Efficiency	Since everything is on plan, the efficiency is high.	The rate is low
Hardware	Sensors, beacons, RFID, etc. other devices to create CPSs	Depends on processes
Internet	Needs for creating CPSs (IoT, IoE, II) internet of things etc.	Internet for internal communication between department and third parties

Compiled from Paschek et al., 2019

The comparison costs between the enterprise adapted the technologies of I5.0 and traditional enterprises are given in Table 2. As a summary, the initial costs (setup, investing devices) are high for I 5.0 but while thinking the long term operating costs (less operator, less error rate and high efficiency & productivity) the costs amount will be less than the costs of an enterprise operating with conventional methods.

1.2. Cybernetics and Self Regulating Systems

Cybernetic is the science of arguing that each animals, machines, social systems more broadly all alive and inanimate systems can communicate, share data among each other and so that they can regulate/manage themselves (Umpleby, 2008). The roots of cybernetic comes from 1940s. In 1947, Norbert Wiener firstly mentioned cybernetic. After observing environmental systems, she decided that all items in enterprises such as machines, man, robots any objects also can communicate among each other and they may manage for themselves. This may be called as revolution for the days and the general attributes and trends of cybernetic are as follows (Grinin & Grinin 2020):

- The increasing amount of information and its growing complexity;
- Consistent development of the systems' abilities for self-regulation;
- Mass use of artificial materials with new properties
- Application and control of systems and processes of various nature including live material and new levels of organization of matter (up to nanoparticles as building blocks)
- Miniaturization trend in many spheres of application (mechanisms, electronic devices, implants, etc.)
- Ubiquitous resource and energy saving
- Individualization and personalization as technological trend

- Humanization of smart technologies and their functions (e.g., voice and gesture interfaces)
- Control to mitigate the negative impacts of human behaviors and activities.

Cybernetics and Industry 4.0&5.0 has a close relationship in those attributes:

- Self-regulating systems
- Smart Technologies
- Artificial intelligence
- Machine learning
- Energy harvesting
- Producing synthetic raw materials.

Hence, it is possible to say Cybernetic is served as a basis for most of today's technological advancements.

1.3. Product Lifecycle Management in Industry 5.0

Product Lifecycle Management (PLM) is the business activity of managing, in the most effective way, a company's products all the way across their lifecycles; from the very first idea for a product all the way through until it is retired and disposed of. The important point in PLM is monitoring data flow by all users in the system at each stage (Stark et al, 2015). This is possible with various seven suitable software and by digitalization in each processes. In new generation production, approach block chain has an important role. Because in block chain every stakeholder has a right to monitor overall process and interpret the operations overall. Thus, PLM approach helps enterprises to reach 5.0 revolutions and its requirement effectively and quickly.

In addition to all it should also mentioned that consumption trends are different before. Designs and product ideas are to be out of date quickly; product life cycle is very short. Today enterprises should make digital transformation in order to achieve agility and flexibility. Hence, they will monitor and manage their processes from end to end simultaneously. In addition, digital transformation help them to reach personalization trends.

1.4. Socio Technique Systems

In I4.0, the previous revolution, smart enterprises, smarts factories, that machines, robots and all entities in it can communicate among each other via internet of things and manage and regulate itself without or very less human intervention. In this approach, the "man" is in the secondary role. Whereas I5.0 bring back socio-technique approach to agenda again.

Socio-technique system term was firstly emerged in England n 1960s. There were so many experiment in coal mining industry. One of them was getting new technologies to mine and observing the results. The results showed that of course new style of doing work, with new technologies, increased the productivity and jobs can finished in a very short time (Trist, 1981, s: 7). Whereas the communication, collaboration and harmony among workers decreased and hence the motivation of workers decreased significantly. Before the introduction of new technologies, mineworkers could communicate and help each other this old system was called as social system. The technique of the systems can also explained as, self but artificially regulating (without human interventions), forecasted, can programmed, and learned from enterprise experience. Socio-technique system theory investigate the man and technology interaction and how technology affect the man in the system (Appelbaum, 1997; Van Dam, 2012: 3). In socio-technique system, enterprise is determined as unit of analysis. Theory focused on man-enterprise interaction and ecosystem as an internal and external environment (Appelbaum, 1997).

Unlike autonomous system, socio-technique systems are the systems where man involved the system in some of the processes and decision point (Geels, 2004). The main point here man has an important roles in arts, handcraft, design and creativity etc. areas in smart enterprise even though existence of digital and autonomous system.

As a summary socio- technique system has such attributes:

- Man and technology work together

- Man can effected from the technological changes in the system

- Organizations are not only mechanical entities, they are also living organisms.

Although Socio-Technique Theory has emerged in 1960s, as of today it is acceptable to think technology as an independent variable. However, in today technology comparable with man intelligence such as artificial intelligence and robots, deep learning etc. cannot be accepted as independent variables. Those technologies and man are working in an interactive ecosystem in new revolution... Both sides can considered as dependent and independent variables depending the dynamic conditions. However, the philosophy is working with advanced Technologies but only for human help and needs. Technology is a servant not master may be no?

Since I5.0 says, it is yes. The technology will exist for the human needs and help him out. They can work in a harmony and collaboratively. The main principles are working together, collaboratively. All systems needs human creativity so there is man in the system in I5.0. Otherwise, the system will be uncompleted.

1.5. Industry 5.0 & Society 5.0

Human development cycle is rather unique but gradual. It takes thousands of years for humans to come this far, yet one might argue that a quick look back of shoulders may reveal how far the distance and how limited the civilizational progress.

The social development can be summarized chronically like this:

- Society 1.0: Hunting & Gathering Society
- Society 2.0: Agricultural Society
- Society 3.0: industry Society
- Society 4.0: information Society
- Society 5.0: Super Smart Society

When Society 1.0 is hunting and gathering society, in society 2.0 man leaved caves, started to live in settled society and engaged in farming. In Society 3.0 man used machines and mass production started. In Society 4.0, humanity used the power of information and o power of hold it and the term has opened Information Society. In Society 5.0, the man intelligence transfer to the machines and robots by man controlled man-machine-robots working ecosystem has created. The main object is to build Super Smart Society (Harayama, 2020). In this society 5.0 is mentioned as a philosophy to help elderly for improving quality of lives and to integrate citizens to new World order.

This new Industrial Revolution called society 5.0 because of serving Technologies for the help of people and reach them. By this way, all people can integrate to the system. Technology is not a threat it is for helping to people, to work for people, to work with people. Man's creativity and robots' speed and accuracy come together and as a result, the productivity, speed and consistency will increased respectively (European Economic and Social Committee, 2020).

By this way, the super smart individual transforms to a super smart society (Sönmez & Suzuki, 2019). Hence, information can be reached, collected, used by everyone objectively.

While societies has adapted I4.0 and technologies come with it, society 5.0 tend in Japan started to direct the World in a very new aspect. S 5.0, firstly mentioned in CeBIT fair in Hannover by Japan's former Prime Minister Mr. Abe, is the philosophy of to integrate older people to society by means of technology (https://www.endustri40.com/endustri-4-0dan-toplum-5-0a/, 01.12.2020).term also called as I5.0 of scholars and practices. The both term and their philosophy based on man-technology integration, collaboration and harmony…

The smart enterprises with self-regulating with robots, machines, artificial intelligence and as a result self-regulating smart enterprises idea comes with I4.0 is changed with I5.0. Because in I5.0 the smart enterprises cannot be without man. The focus is Human in I5.0. It establish and maintain technology for the sake of human help. In reality I5.0 term also called by scholars as "Augmented Age" (Longo et al, 2020). Since man and machines work in collaboratively to help and increase capability of man, the performance and capability of man is augmented. Augmented operators, augmented human capability, augmented cognitive capability, augmented reality etc. some other terms are emerged with this revolution. I5.0 soften the mechanic phenomenon comes with previous revolution such as enterprises without man, controlled and managed by robots, machines and artificial intelligence. Conversely I4.0 in I5.0 man is in the focused design, cognitive, analytical processes controlled and managed by man while other repetitive and monotone processes controlled and done by robots, machines; by mechanic parts of organization.

By means of I5.0 the World, transfer from the information society to the smart society. Using artificial intelligence, advanced robots and internet of everything in everywhere the super smart Society will be created.

However, the rigidity of technological dominance in I4.0, I5.0 approach is keener to socio-technic system (Wang, 2019). I5.0 is faced with the new paradigm change such as:

- Management with artificial intelligence
- Internet for everything, everyone and everywhere
- After 5G, the speed of process will increased visibly.
- Humanoid and collaborative robots increase the interaction between man-robots

Doing most of the repetitive jobs from robots.

THE COMPONENTS OF I 5.0

2. THE MAIN COMPONENTS OF INDUSTRY 5.0

Following technological changes and transformation realized with i4.0, the World is ready for upcoming revolution; collaborative robots, artificial intelligence, renewable resources, enables to reach and manage enterprises from everywhere and any time, digital economy, new type of currencies (crypto), bioeocomy, artificial gen technology, biotechnology the World has ready for new transformation: I5.0.

I 5.0 follows same steps as I4.0, its attributes are:

- End-to-end Digital Integration
- Vertical Integration
- Horizontal Integration
- Machine-to-Machine Communication

End-to-End Digital Integration (E2E): End-to-end integration is networking and integrating all the value chain while facilitating to have every single terminal in the system digital signal (Zhou, Liu & Zhou, 2015).

Vertical Integration: It refers to integrating internal systems in the enterprise such as ERP (Enterprise Resource Planning), PLM (Product Lifecycle Management), MES (Management Executive Systems) and MOM (Manufacturing Operating System)

Horizontal Integration: Integration of all information system between producer, distributers, suppliers, consumers and third parties to facilitate work together seamlessly. Thus, form supplier to customer's data flow will be realized (Crnjac, Veza and Banduka, 2017).

Vertical and horizontal integration terms showed in Figure 6.

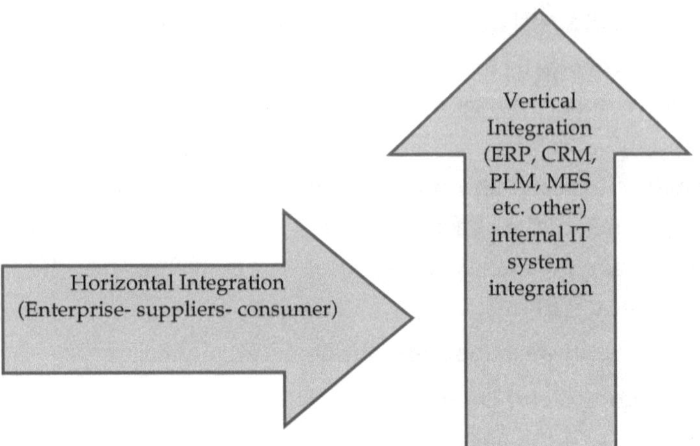

Figure 6. Vertical vs. Horizontal Integration

Horizontal integration means is networking all the parties in the production processes digitally via internet. However, vertical integration means more internal integration by means of integration of software's such as ERP, MES, PLM, CRM etc.

Machine to Machine Communication (M2MC): By the help of internet of things every object can be connect to internet communicate each other. All machines and objects are communicate each other by means of internet and smart sensors.

I 5.0 is focused to make production by means of the use of; artificial intelligence, collaborative robots, bio economy, very high speed internet and processes with the help of man-robots-machines collaboration. The main components of I5.0 shown in Figure 7.

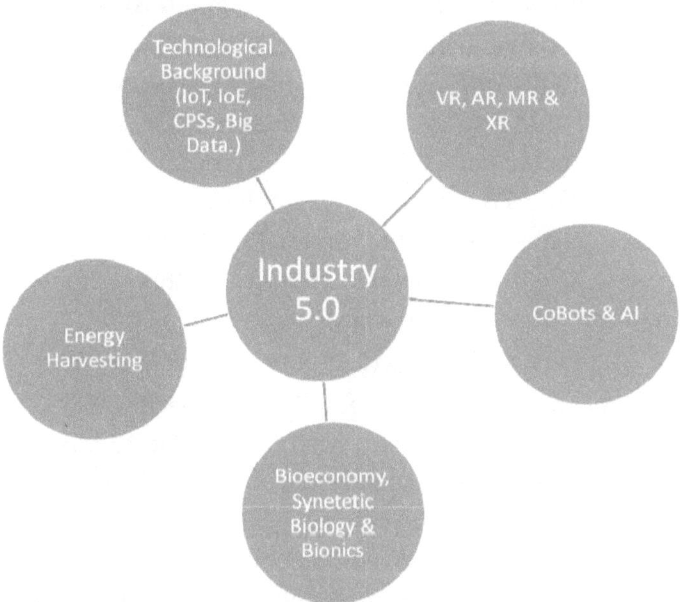

Figure 7. The Main Components of I5.0

As shown in Figure 7. The main components of I5.0 are follows:

- Technological background
- Collaborative robots & Artificial intelligence
- Biotechnology, Synthetic Biology &Bionics
- VR, AR, MR & XR
- Energy harvesting

In addition of I4.0 technological components, collaborative robots, artificial intelligence, and internet for everything, digital bio economy and biotechnology are the main subjects comes with I5.0. Since I5.0 use some of the technologies used in I4.0, the main principles and technological background of I4.0 will be mentioned here.

2.1. The Technological Background of Industry 5.0

The main logic behind I5.0 is also digitalization and to enhance self-regulating systems. In order to achieve these goal enterprises should create CPS in the system from end to end. The main components of CPSs are IoT, IoE, and 5G, sensors etc. after creation of CPS the other step is collecting and analyzing big data and computing them. Virtual Reality and other subjects related to new technologies also use I5.0. In this section of book, technological background of I5.0 will be explained.

2.1.1. Internet of Things (IoT) & Internet of Everything (IoE)

IoT means that making feasible to connecting object to the internet. The main logic is connecting the object to internet with embedded devices on it. With the sake of IoT, object can be sensed and reached from networks, controlled (Williams, 2014). Thus, managing every objects such as; machines, robots and even man, can be possible from networks. By IoT, physical systems can be transformed to smart and cyber physical systems (Sanders, et al, 2016).

Figure 8. IOT

Jackkdanial, 15.01.2021 (Wikimedia)

IoT term firstly emerged in 1982. The vending machines were equipped with devices facilitate the machine to connect the internet. The machines were useful for those days to report some of the information such as the amount of cokes in the machines, their level of coldness etc. (Farooq, Mazhar, Khairi & Kamal, 2015).

IoT has four layers. They are (Da Xu, He &Li, 2014):

- Sensing Layer

- Networking Layer

- Service Layer

- Interface Layer

Table 3. The Layers of IOT

Layers	Description
Sensing layer	This layer is integrated with existing hardware (RFID, sensors, actuators etc.) to sense/control the physical World and acquire data
Networking Layer	Networking Layer provides basic networking support and data transfer over wireless or wired network
Service Layer	Service Layer creates and manages services. It provides services to satisfy user needs
Interface Layer	Interface Layer, provides interaction methods to users and other applications

Da Xu, 2014

Industrial Internet of Thing IIoT is another term derived from IoT and used especially for manufacturing industries. IIoT is the quite simple application of IoT for industrial machines, vehicles, robots any other industrial devices (Boyes et al, 2018).

There can be mentioned so many application of IoT. Today especially in health sector the wearable technologies are the main IoT application. By these technologies, the MD (doctor) can monitor the all relevant information about patients in real time. Rhythm, body temperature, cholesterol level, possible heart attach can be monitored by the help of wearable devices & internet: IoT.

Case Study
To be on Schedule even on traffic congestion. A solution for a bus driver in Osnabrück. In below we will see the simple solution developed for a bus driver. He want to be on time but at somehow in bus stops it is not always possible to pulling back after stopping in the bus stops especially in the city center. Here are the IOT solution for a bus driver:
"Otto works for the municipality of Osnabrück. He is employed as a bus driver. He manages bus line 1. Line 1's route ranges from the central train station in the middle of the city to a nearby village in the south of Osnabrück, 10 km from the city center. Especially at the bus stops in the city, the bus has a hard time pulling back out into traffic after stopping. This of course results in wasted time and delays in Otto's usual route. In addition to the simple usage of indicator lights, an application is planned that informs nearing cars about the starting bus. Karl, driving a car behind the stopping bus, gets a notification (acoustical/visual) on his navigation system/smartphone that the bus will leave the bus stop any moment. Karl can react early and reduce the speed of his car giving Otto the opportunity to get back into traffic. Hence, the bus can stay on schedule."

https://iot.ieee.org/iot-scenarios.html?prp=oc-1cc8f9b7-1a3f-46f3-8cf2-7167045fd2cc, 01.08.2020

Another application of IoT is for home solutions, smart homes. In smart homes, you can control the heat, humidity, lights, coffee etc. from your office. Smart traffic, smart cities is the other mostly used application of IoT. However, the most widespread application and accepted as equivalent term as I4.0 is smart factories and enterprises in where cyber physical system has created.

Internet of Services-IoS: In IoS not internet of people but enterprises are on the focuse. IoS go far beyond web services and is aim to facilitate also for non-professionals to help them to create their contents, trade (Cardoso, Winkler, Voigt& Berthold, 2009).

Internet of Everything (IoE): After 5G Technologies, the speed of internet has increased enormously and accessibility from everywhere even desert on roads are possible. IoE means connecting and maintain communication among every man, machines, robots, things as a generally every item and object in the system.

2.1.2. 5G-Cellular Network Technologies

1G, 2G, 2.5 G, 3G, 3.75G, 4,5G and lastly 5G: 5th generation of GSM technology. With 5G Technologies comparing to the last generations of GSM, the speed of data transfer is very high and the latency is decreased by the help of deploying so many sensors and challenge of communication technologies and data mining (Wang, et al., 2018).

Comparing to the 4G with 5G (Wu et al., 2017; Hossain & Hassan, 2015):

- System capacity increase by x1000
- Spectral efficiencyx10
- 5G uses also energy harvesting methods and uses the remaining energy in the system
- increase the energy efficiency
- Cellular Throughputx25.

This new type of technology not only between people to people but also between people to machine, machine to machine and anywhere, anytime and by means of any device (anyhow) communication is possible (C.X Wang et al., 2014).

Comparing to the last generations 5G has a software base. This means that, all of the controls and managerial processes in the network can possibly done by means of softwares (Yılmaz, 2019). This facilitates to access and control the network simultaneously.

To increase in number of mobile Technologies and devices means that increase in mobile data traffic. Games played on mobile devices, watched videos, like sharing photographs and big files etc. increase the data density. To solve these problems operators try to decrease the volume of cellular data. In this way the amount of data transferred from cell to cell will decreased and spectral efficiency will increase (Chin, Fan& Haines, 2014). Data traffic will decrease, speed will increase and capacity will increase properly.

This type of cells can be pico (small) and macro. The combination of these cells created heterogeneous networks. In conventional system, there is only one network but in heterogeneous cells, there are more one small heterogonous cells (Hossain &Hassan, 2015). This type of network is called Heterogeneous Typology.

To successes in IOT, as main components of I5.0 there are listings are the main requirements:

- High speed internet infrastructure,
- High capacity for rapid data computing and store big data,
- As possible as low latency
- Appropriate and powerful ecosystem for huge sensors, servers, devices connected to internet and communicate each other.

Since 5G technology facilitate high-speed internet in everywhere with low latency and in high-density data transfer ecosystem it can be concluded it is the important components of I5.0.

5G-Intelligent internet of Things (I-IoT): 5G I-IoT is the new term that combines smart systems with IoT. It aimed to compute big data and optimize communication channels with big data mining, deep learning, reinforcement learning techniques (Wang, et al., 2018).

2.1.3. Cyber-Physical System-(CPS)

Cyber Physical Systems are name of the ecosystem that every objects are equipped with devices and sensors for connecting internet. The main logic is behind CPS to transfer all objects, machines, devices in physical system to the virtual environment. Thus to control and monitor the system virtually. In this system, data are gathered by smart sensors and the big data environment is created in the cyber physical system. (Kang, et al., 2016).

2.1.4. Big Data

Big data is the term that describes the huge amount of data that cannot be used and analyzed in conventional data computing methods (Kang et al., 2016). Since every objects, machines and devices connected to the internet and all of type of communications among them are virtually managed and realized via internet as a result the amount of data transmitted to the servers will be also huge. Big data stand for this type of huge amounts of data.

Big data Technologies facilitate to analysis of unstructured data and to created data oriented models (Isaksson, Harjunkoski & Sand, 2018). Thus, the customers' demands and consumption pattern can be forecasted.

2.1.5. Cloud Computing

Cloud computing are the system of store and analyzed big data. In this type of technology, so many servers are combined under the cloud and facilitate to communicate and make possible to data transfer between each other (Rao, Saluia, Sharma, Mittal & Sharma, 2012).

Remote sensing systems and smart sensors: smart sensor have important roles in I4.0 and 5.0. Especially the systems are requires smart sensors from machine to machine communication and interaction between man- machine.

To connecting objects to the internet are done with some of the equipment. As mentioned before the objects only can connect the internet that embedded of assembling appropriate device. Similarly, sensing and perception of this equipped object and perception it by other object in the system is possible for using smart sensors.

2.1.6. Mixed Reality-MR, Virtual Reality-VR, Augmented Reality-AR & Extended Reality-XR

In this part of the book mixed, virtual, augmented, extended reality will be explained.

<u>Mixed Reality- MR</u>

Mixed reality firstly mentioned by Paul Milgram and Fumio Kishino in 1994. The mixed reality term can be defined as virtual and real life objects comes together within an interactive real time environment (Billinghurst & Kato, 1999).

According to Milgram's reality–virtuality continuum, MR is compromise the real and virtual environment and objects at the same time on Virtual Reality Continuum Scala shown in Figure 9. (Azuma, Bailot, Behringer & Julier & MacIntyre, 2001).

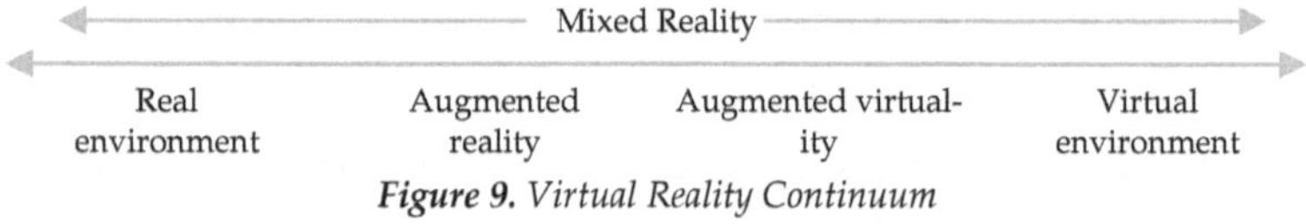

Figure 9. Virtual Reality Continuum

Azuma et al., 2001

Augmented Virtuality and Augmented Reality are the subsets lying within the Mixed Reality range of the Reality-Virtuality (RV) continuum (Dunston & Wang, 2011).

Virtual Reality-VR

Virtual reality term, the subject lying within a mixed reality. In virtual reality in another term artificial reality, there is a synthetic World for users (Carmigniani et al., 2011). The real world tries to imitate and understand via virtual objects.

VR has so many applications especially in manufacturing and construction has widespread operations in many areas. By VR the operations held in a more reliable environment with a less error and data flow among each user such as suppliers, producers, designers (Dawood, Marasini & Dean, 2008).

VR has four components: software, hardware, input and output devices. The software essentially is a set of mathematical algorithms and equations that define the virtual environment and its responses to the interactions with the user. The hardware is needed to perform the great number of calculations required by the software to produce the rapidly changing virtual environment. Input devices are the cameras, Mouse, keyboard, voice recognition devices and any other input devices. Output device are the VR head mounted displays (glasses) (Dawood, Harter & Krummel, 2002).

Augmented Reality- AG

Augmented Reality (AR) is derived from VR. It facilitates to make more understandable of virtual environment by enriching it. AR allows the user to see the real world, with virtual objects superimposed upon or composited with the real world. Therefore, AR supplements reality, rather than completely replacing it (Azuma, 1997). Chronologic development of AR is shown in Figure 10.

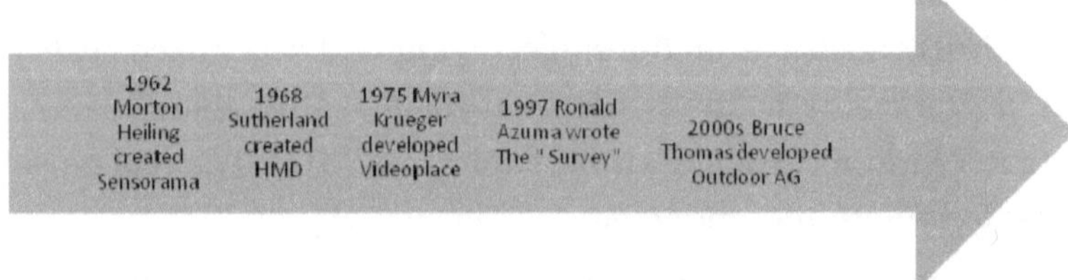

Figure 10. The History of AR

compiled from Alkhamisi, et al., 2013

Figure 10 shows us the first development in AR is sensorama device created by Morton Heiling in 1962. Sensorama stimulate the hearing, seeing, smelling and touching senses and facilitate to see the objects in three dimensions. Thus, users have experience to see the objects as if it is in real environment. Since sensorama and other Works of Morton did not understand and accepted by authorizes he worked in other areas (Britannica, 2020).

After Morton's' scientific contribution to AR, Ivan Sutherland who was worked in Sutherland Bell Laboratories in this days, published is scientific article named "Ultimate Display". In this article, Sutherland focused the importance of monitor technology in virtual imagination. He emphasis monitor technology is the main variable to higher quality and reality of virtual images. He is the first scientist to created head mounted glass (CSAIL, 2020).

In 1975 we can see Krueger working in this field with his working "Videoplace". He wanted to create an environment that surrounded users and monitor/follow their movement. After following their movement without any contributor such as head mounted displays, gloves any type of wearable devices, the movement will be digitalized to percept and respond their movement   (https://aboutmyronkrueger.weebly.com/video-place.html, 26.01.2020).

After his colleagues Azuma published, his first article in 1997 mentioned the augmented reality. This article is the most cited article in those days. He is the first one who mentioned augmented reality, the state of the art term. The importance of this article is the systematic and principles of AR is explained briefly in it (Azuma, 2016).

The adjacent development in AR is followed by creation of play named "ARQuake". In ARQuake you can walk freely in a physical space while playing this game. With this game people walk freely in the outdoor and the images can be adjusted depending on the glasses-head mounted display weared on head (Piekarski &Thomas, 2002).

AR is the variation of virtual reality. Since in virtual reality is an artificial environment, in AR, the environment is enrichment with real World objects also. The augmented term means that the images, videos, voice records created artificially. In other words, the artificial contents, objects is added to the real environment, mixed and blended. Other methods is the addition virtual environment to the real alive videos (Bimber & Raskar, 2005). There are the attributes of AR (Azuma, 1997):

- Real and virtual environment is being together

- There exists real World interaction

- Real and virtual images are registered in three dimensions.

By means of AR, objects can be realized, seen, smelled, heard and may be tasted them different from the real World (Van Krevelen & Poclman, 2010).

Apart from them, the new term emerged in this field: Augmented Virtuality. In AV, virtual environment is enriched with real World data (Tamura, Yamamoto &Katayama, 2001).

AR has so many applications in tourism. While visiting a touristic destination it is possible to gathered information even restoration information and it is possible to create a route depending your destination that tour in (Vlahakis et.al., 2001).

There is also new type of AR: Hybrid 4-Dimensional Augmented Reality (HD4AR). HD4AR is facilitate for gathering data from any pictures with its contents sensitive AR applications from any place (Bae, Golparvar-Fard & White, 2013). With the help of HD4AR, it is possible achieve, monitor, manage to any personnel, machines etc. easily. While thinking big any big Project like construction helded in a very huge space it is helpful for to prevent any misunderstanding and communication error. HD4AR is helpful while thinking any big manufacturing facilities or trip in a touristic destination. The process, man, machine can be controlled and directed easily without being physically in the real space.

There are three types of AR display devices. They are hand mounted displays let's say AR glasses, handheld displays and spatial displays (Zhou, Duh & Billinghust, 2008):

- Head mounted displays: It is created by Ivan Sutherland in 1966. It is named as its shape as sword of Democles (Information, 2020). Today's developing Technologies facilitate to make possible to change image or to engage the virtual environment by only finger, eye movements without using Mouse or any other input devices.

- Handheld Displays: As named handheld displays, it is hand monitor. It is secondly the most used display devices after hand mounted displays. They are mobile phones, tablets and personal digital assistant-PDAs (Wagner & Schmalstieg, 2006).

- Spatial Displays: In Spatial Augmented Reality (SAR), make use of video-projectors, optical elements, holograms, radio frequency tags, and other tracking technologies to display graphical information directly onto physical objects without requiring the user to wear or carry the display (Carmigniani et al., 2011).

AR is classified in to three groups as its user interface and interaction levels: tangible, collaborative and Hybrid AR (Feng, Duh & Billinghurst, 2008).

- Tangible AR: digital data are manipulated by physical devices in Tangible User Interface (TUSs) ARs.

- Collaborative AG: In collaborative Augmented Reality multiple users may access a shared space populated by virtual objects, while remaining grounded in the real world (Kaufmann, 2003).

- Hybrid AR: It is the combination of TUIs AR and Hybrid AR.

<u>Extended Reality-XR</u>

XR is the new term mixing and combining Virtual, Augmented and MR together. Figure 11 shows the relationship of VR, AR, MR and XR.

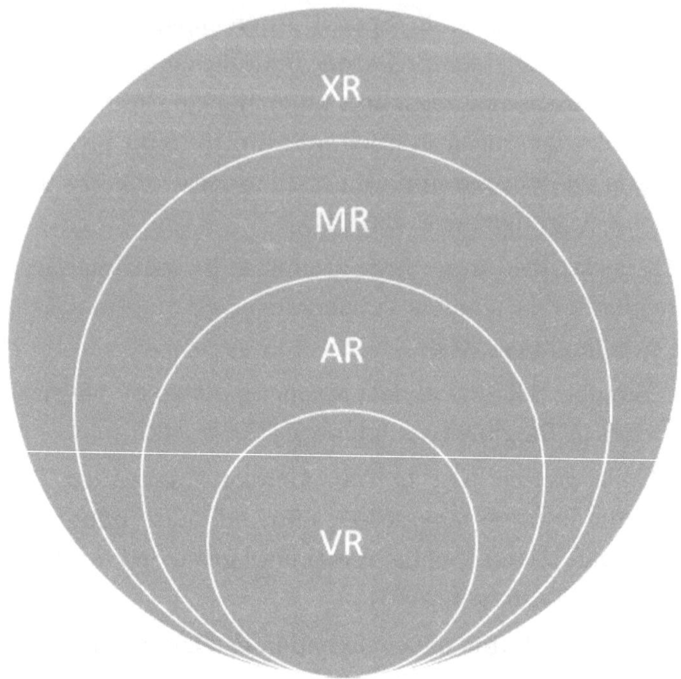

Figure 11. The Relationship between XR, MR, AR & VR

As Figure 11, shows the XR include all the other types of virtual reality forms. All types of XR, MR, AR and VR are close relationship with I5.0 like listed below:

- Creates simulated environments to show researchers a path and minimize the errors in real life
- Facilitate to make Works quickly and timely
- Decrease the orientation time for new person started job in enterprises
- Make possible to engage customers in the processes at the beginning of the design.

There is also Holograms can be defined under VR and AR subjects. Hologram technology can be described as transferring objects into a virtual environment as a 3D and virtually with the help of VR and AR. The term by itself is the combination of two Greek words as a whole view- Holos and written- gram (Ghuloum, 2010). The technology developed by Gabor in 1947 (Mastrangelo & Team).

This technology is used today in medical education, automotive industry in design processes. The logic of hologram technology can be described in there steps (Ghloum, 2010):

- Hologram technology can be described as transferring objects into a virtual environment as a 3D and virtually with the help of VR and AR. The term by itself is the combination of two Greek words as a whole view- Holos and written- gram (Ghuloum, 2010). The technology developed by Gabor in 1947 (Mastrangelo & Team). Light source is projected into the surface of the objects and scattered

- The second light illuminated the object and create interference between both sources

- The two light sources interact with each other and cause diffraction, which appears as a 3D image.

2.1.7. Artificial Intelligent (AI)

This term is emerged also in I4.0. AI is simulating the human behavior and brain algorithms (Paschou, Adrodegari, Rapaccini, Saccani & Perona, 2018). Since the interaction with human and non-humanoid object in, I 5.0 artificial intelligence becomes more and more important subject than ever. The interaction attributes, requesting the orders and giving answers to the questions, solving problems by itself and make decision to the overall ongoing processes are the main functions of robots donated with artificial intelligence. These processes can be successful with the help of machine learning, deep learning some other algorithms.

Machine Learning is the computer programming to summarize and make understandable statistical result from the big data. It transforms the inputs of an algorithm into outputs using statistical, data-driven rules that are automatically derived from a large set of examples, rather than being explicitly specified by humans (Estava, et al., 2014). In this book, only supervised and unsupervised MLAlgorith (MLA) will be explained.

In supervised MLA, researchers has data and known result of these data. Researcher enter the data and the result and try to make logical result from a given data. In other words, by this way researcher teach or force to learn algorithm to guess meaningful result from a given data set. Thus, the experimental relationship between input and result is established (Kılınç & Başeğmez, 2018). In unsupervised MLA, researcher work with huge data sets and try to inference meaningful result from given data (Alpaydın, 2020).

Deep learning is another algorithm to analyze and understanding data get the latent pattern from huge data. The working principle is very similar with machine learning but in deep learning; there is more than one layer. However, the machine learning there is only one layer. In deep learning all the layers are on the progress at the same time.

In Deep Learning Algorithm (DLA) there are layers that ordered in hierarchical rules. Each layer pull the result of lower layer and use it as the input (Şeker, Diri & Balık, 2017). Deep-learning methods are representation-learning methods with multiple levels of representation, obtained by composing simple but non-linear modules that each transform the representation at one level (starting with the raw input) into a representation at a higher, slightly more abstract level (LeCun, Benio & Hinton, 2015). In other words, DLA try to inference an understandable and logical result from the raw data. It Works with so many data sets and try to find the best result. Those data can be images, videos, sounds and even speech files. Face recognition systems and virtual assistant in mobile phones are the applications of DLA.

The applications of DLA is so many such as autonomous cars and smart traffics. Smart traffics applications such as autonomous cars, accident, traffic light and road conditions controls. Smart city applications such as; water, electricity and weather forecast controls.an also wearable clothes. The big data collected by wearable clothes and analyzed by the help of DLA and other machine-learning algorithm it is facilitated to control diseases, heart attack and any type of health problems (Hatcher & Yu, 2018).

By the help of IoT CPSs are collected big data. It is impossible to analyzed and monitor it simultaneously by conventional methods. Time limit and to develop a simultaneous solutions is force to enterprises to use DLAs. Since its capacity and ability to find solutions from huge data simultaneously, DLA is a very helpful tool also in I 5.0.

2.1.8. 3 D, 4D and 5D Printers

After three Dimension (3D) printers emerged in our Daily life, fast, easy and with less cost production mentality is also come into question. 3D printers facilitate to manufacture very complicated parts with only a few materials. 3D printers are mostly used in AM production processes (Turkey Industry 4.0 Platform, 2020)

4Dimensions printers has also three dimension as in 3D printers and addition X,Y, Z coordinates there is also T coordinates which shows the time. I means that objects can be change timely (Li, Shang & Wang, 2017). The differences between three and 4 D printers are showed in Table 4.

Table 4. The Differences between 3D and 4D

	3D	4D
Dimensions	3 D; X,Y,Z	4 D; X,Y,Z and T (time)
Materials used	Depends on the process and product	Smart Materials
Time sensivity	No	Yes, can change with in a time

Quanjin et al., (2020).

As summarized in Table 4. The main difference is time dimension between two types of printers. There is also another important difference is the type of material used in both printers. In 4D printers, the material is smart and can change over time. This means that materials are sensitive to a time and can changed over time and under different circumstances (Pei, 2014). For example when the weather get warm or cold the material can be stretched in order prevent fragility of the product. In some cases pressure, atmosphere, temperature, gravity etc. are other different conditions that might be considered as a changeable over time.

On the other hand, it is not mentioned in Table 4 the other differences between 3D and 4 D printers are smooth geometric surface of the finished product. In 3D printers the finished product need to retouch after the manufacturing processes but in, 4D printer's surface of the finished product is more smooth and nearly there is no need to retouch or any other smoothing processes.

Five Dimension (5D) printers are the printers that has three dimensions and five axes. In 5D, printers very complicated devices. Products are manufactured by less materials and being done properly. Also in 5D, printers more agile and durable product are manufactured (Asif et al., 2018). The smoothness is also better comparing to the other two types of (3 and 4D) printers.

2.1.9. Additive Manufacturing (AM)

Additive Manufacturing (AM) is transforming 3D models (Computer Aided Design-CAD files) to physical products. In this technology, materials are combined and sintered with the help of ultrasonic waves, and laser lights or electron lights (Campbell, Bourell & Gibson, 2012). In other words, AM, is the production of new age, production from materials by layer layer by control of computers with the help of printers. (Knofius, Van der Heijden & Zijm, 2016). AM mentality emerged after 3D printers technology was entered our life, especially from design stage the preparation of prototype (Rapid Prototyping-RP) in each stage AM.

AM, is also named as additive fabrication, additive processes, additive techniques, additive layer manufacturing, layer manufacturing, freeform fabrication, rapid manufacturing (Alcisto et al., 2011, Levy, Schindel & Kruth, 2003).

AM production technologies differs from the materials used in the processes as, powder, liquid and solid form (Aktimur & Gökpınar, 2015; Melchels et al., 2012). Liquid based AM production methods are:

- Stereo lithography
- Jetting Systems
- Direct Light Processing
- High Viscosity Jetting.

Powder based AM production methods are:

- Selective Laser Sintering
- Direct Metal Laser Sintering
- 3D Printing

- Fused Metal Deposition Systems
- Electron Beam Melting
- Selective Laser Melting
- Selective Inhibition Sintering
- Electro photographic Layered Manufacturing
- High Speed Sintering

Solid based AM production methods are:

- Sheet Stacking Technology
- Fused Deposition Modelling (Aktimur & Gökpınar, 2015; Melchels et al., 2012).

Systematically AM processes can be explained like followings (Huang, Liu, Mokasdar & Hou, 2013):

- 3D solid model will be designed and transform to the STL format which is the file format that AM machines/printers uses.
- Files send to the AM machines and positioning setups are make
- Production layer by layer has started.

Applications of AM is not limited by manufacturing industries. AM type of production and printers are using in especially to satisfy the food demand of astronauts in space. This type of production is now widespread using to preparation pastas, sandwiches and either chocolates with very complicated geometric shapes (Lipton, Cutler, Nigl, Cohen & Lipson, 2015).

AM, helps to increase the speed of manufacturing processes and facilitate to using light materials. In AM, it is possible to create very complicated products from an only one materials and in a one piece (Additively, 2020; GE Turkey, 2020).

With the help of AM enterprises can (Kruth, Leu & Nakagawa, 1998):

- Product quickly and efficiently
- Design and make prototype quickly
- Work with a very few material
- Control the processes easily
- Decrease the amount of scraps
- To transform the processes depending to the principle of I 4.0.

Today it is impossible to say that AM completely substitutes conventional manufacturing processes. When thinking 3D printers and raw materials used in these printers prices are so high it will cost too much for and ordinary enterprises. Besides prices, also surface of the finished product is another disadvantage of AM. There is no smooth surface finished products in AM. There should also be retouch after printers finished its job. In addition, personnel that knows this technology and can control the machines are not so much and not so much skilled. When once gather all disadvantages of AM in today's technology it cannot be replaced conventional manufacturing but might be a part of manufacturing processes.

Although there are so many disadvantage of AM explained before, Am also is the future and part of today's technology unless technological development in AM machines and materials. If cost of materials and machines will be declined and speed of machines are increase, output amount also increase and thus overall cost will be declined. Under these conditions, AM will be considered as today's technology.

AM has so many advantage comparing to the conventional production. With the help of AM, preparation of prototype and production speed will be increased. Thus, high speed, and flexible production aim of the I 5.0 will be achieved. Also since production processes are digitally controlled, managed and realized a very few may be no manipulation will be done.

2.2. Robots & Collaborative Robots-CoBots & Artificial Intelligence (AI)

From industry to the social life, robots are being the main assistant of our daily life. Armed with artificial intelligence, virtual and augmented reality and machine learning robots are becoming the main components of I5.0.

When the robots were developed and produced for the first time, they (I3.0) had only two main functions: navigation and manipulation. Navigator robots were mapping the area that are watched and traced by cameras and laser scanners. In order to do this job they were turning around/walking in the related area autonomously. Manipulation duty that held by robots is a functioning like human arm (Kanda & Ishiguro, 2017). Robot are being used in manufacturing industry replacing the most to the operator's jobs.

The advantage of working with robots re (Ozkeser, 2018):

- Enterprises can obtain more acure and reliable results with working robots
- The quality of the processes and products will be increased
- They can achieve the optimum cost goals
- They can save their operators from high risks and work accidents
- Robots can report about the ongoing processes and about the duality of the process simultaneously. Hence, the optimization in each processes can be ensured.

Todays, robots have more function than the robot arms. Robots are now designing like human assistant to make movements like human and has social duties like speaking and communicating with people.

There are so many robotic Technologies. Sony has created AIBO. AIBO is a dog and can shake human hands, when you make eye contact and order it do its jobs, can sit and stand up, eating is also sensitive to touching and as a result it behave like real dog (AIBO, 2020).

From 2003 until at the end of to 2006, Sony worked on a Qrio Project. In this Project, they were working on humanoid robots. Qrio can hear, walk, singing, running, dancing, recognize people and also can grasp the objects (IEEE, 2020).

Mitsubishi is created Wakamaru. Wakamaru has three functions; to contact and be friends with people; it can make eye contact and serve people (Shiotani et al., 2006).

Asimo is created in 1986 as first humanoid robots. Assimo can climb ladder, turn the light off, step forward and backward like any human. It is created for the sake of human help and to assistant them (Honda, 2020). By developing humanoid robots elders, disabled, kids care any other human care can be done with robots.

Figure 12. Asimo "The Humanoid Robot"
https://honda.com.tr/asimo, 9.08.2020.

Tourism industry has also using robots like; tour guide in museum named: Rhino, Minerva, Sage, Chips, Care-o-bot,

Hermes, Jinny, Robovie and EnonIndigo, in showrooms named: Robox, Mona (Boboc, Horatiu & Talabâ, 2014; Burgard, Cremes, Fox, Hahnel, Lakemeyer, Schulz, Steiner & Thrun, 1998; Nourbakhsh, Bobenage, Grange, Lutz, Meyer & Soto, 1999).

Robots can classified in to two groups as industrial and social robots. According to the ISO, industrial robots can be explained like this (ISO, 2020):

"Industrial Robots can automatically controlled, reprogrammable (2.4), multipurpose (2.5)manipulator (2.1), programmable in three or more axes (4.3), which can be either fixed in place or mobile for use in industrial automation applications.

Robots as a Service (RaaS), apart from duties industrial robots has social robots can interact with people and objects and help people."

The number of RaaS and sales volume is very high in today markets. According to the International Federation of Robotics, the sales amount in RaaS in 2018 is increased as %32 and became as 9.2 million in dollars (International Federation of Robotics 2020).

Industrial robots has robot arms and many other functions in manufacturing as mentioned before. However, RaaS has so many social duties can handle like home chores and elderly care. Besides its social Works RaaS has also other industrial duties. They can work as warehouse operators can manage the materials classify and locate them appropriately in a manufacturing enterprises. They are working as autonomous operators far from many core-manufacturing processes. We can also see RaaS in hospitals. For example in Denmark robots can handle and classified blood collection tube (Kuka, 2020). When you think big hospitals, they have thousands sample blood tube, they need more than one operator, and take may be days to classify and organize only sample tubes.

Now we are faced with swarm robotics in I 5.0 in which so many robots let us say *swarm of robots* are acting their job.

2.3. Bio-Economy, Synthetic Biology &Bionics

United Nations (UN) are published 17 principles for sustainable development they are (https://www.un.org/sustainabledevelopment/, 01.12.2020):

- No poverty
- Zero hunger
- Good health and well being
- Quality education
- Gender equality
- Clean water and sanitation
- Affordable and clean energy
- Decent work and economic growth
- Industry, innovation and infrastructure
- Reduced inequality
- Sustainable cities and communities
- Responsible consumption and production
- Climate action
- Life below water
- Life on land
- Peace, justice and strong institutions
- Partnership for the goals.

Figure 13. 17 *Goals for Sustainable Development*
https://www.un.org/sustainabledevelopment/news/communications-
material/, 01.30.2020

While scrutinizing the 17 goals the most of them are related with the clean production for clean environment and World. With these goals, UNs urge to firms and society to balance between environment and production ecosystem and producing like:

- Conserving natural resources
- Using less amount of energy
- Decreasing amount of wastes.

Rethinking UNs 17 goals the new concept is emerged: Bio economy or Bio-Based Economy. Bio based economy can be defined as producing using biological and natural energy resources in manufacturing instead of fuel and also consuming natural and renewal materials in every sectors of the industries (Bugge et al., 2016).

Figure 14. Bio economy
https://ktn-uk.co.uk/news/improving-lives-and-strengthening-our-economy-
a-national-bioeconomy-strategy-to-2030, 01.08.2020.

Although it is, the Pioneer of every country as workings on I4.0 subject Germany has also advice and helps researcher related bio economy. The German Federal Government published a report "National Research Strategy Bio Economy 2030" and the core of actions in this report are given followings (Biotech 2030.ru):

- Global food security
- Sustainable agricultural production
- Healthy and safe foods
- The industrial application of renewable resources
- Increasing use of biomass-based energy.

Thus, Germany wants to take a position for being as the "dynamic research and innovation center for bio-based products, energy, processes and services" (Sachsenmeir, 2016)

Conserving natural resources is the main responsibility of every enterprises as everyone under the circumstances of climate change, natural resources becomes exhausting and environmental pollution reaches up to very high and intolerable levels. While doing these enterprises will be the pioneer to the others in competitive market environment also in I5.0 revolution. Because whether monitoring and managing block chain or high speed and accessible internet with 5G and mobile Technologies consumers are monitoring and tracing the production and in each stage of the value chain and decide to buy or not. Every member of information society is able to monitor transparently, control production in each step, and make buying decision. Hence, enterprises should use renewable resources without harming the environment and satisfy customer's sustainability demands and expectations.

Synthetic Biology and Bionics

Synthetic biology is the redesigning organisms for functional needs by engineering methods to create biological devices, systems and organisms (Weber & Fussenegger, 2012). Synthetic biology is the science dealed with genetically coded organisms and their DNA sequences. In synthetic biology DNA sequence is classified, ordered and redesign depending on demands and requests (Braun &Inhofer, 2014). Thus, in synthetic biology, biological structures redesigned and reproduce synthetically according to the principle to reengineering methods.

Bionic is the process of creation of artificial objects by imitating entities, process there exist in the nature/real life (Grunwald, 2016). Airplanes, spiroid winglets, new car tire are designed like cats' paws, and spiderlike robots with autonomous legs are examples of bionic science (Sachsenmeier, 2016). Bionic eyes, ears, prosthesis etc. are the other applications of bionic in medical sciences. As understand from the examples bionic is the science that can facilitate not only designing stage but also in physical product manufacturing.

2.4. Energy Harvesting

In Cyber physical systems ecosystem that machines, robots, devices etc. are connected and communicated each other and thus system needs plenty of energy. In addition to this, the energy losses can be recovered by cyber objects and can be put back to the circulation within t the system by applying appropriate methods. This method known as energy harvesting.

Energy harvesting is a technique that facilitate to create appropriate sustainable ecosystem for renewable and clean energy production. In this method, the unused and wasted energy is collected and regain to the system use (Tan & Panda, 2010: 3). By doing, this there created an alternative and supplementary energy resources for batteries. The energy resources that are wasted can be recovered with the help of energy harvesting arc listed below (Harb, 2011):

- Sun/solar
- Wind
- Kinetic
- Thermal
- Wearable devices
- Vibration
- Light

2.4.1. The energy harvesting technology

In this method, from the different resource energies are collected and transform into the electric energy. This collection can be via with wire/wireless devices and sensors.

There are so many applications of energy harvesting. The energy collected by the motion of human arms, knees and legs is collection of biomechanics energy one example to the energy harvesting (Choi, Lee & Jeon, 2017). Another example is wearable devices. With the help of wearable devices, thermal energy (the body temperature) is collected and transform to the electric energy (Kim et al., 2014).

Cyber physical systems in I4.0 and I5.0 hundreds of objects connected to the internet and communicate each other thus uses exhaust so many energy resources. Besides, the very important part of the energy is also wasted and freely moving in the ecosystem and should be collected and regain. Hence, energy harvesting is the main important subject in the new industrial revolutions and maybe in the comings.

THE NEW TERMS IN I 5.0

3. THE NEW TERMS EMERGED IN I 5.0

In this part of the book, new terms such as personalization, shared and gig economy, crowdsourcing and social manufacturing will be explained

3.1. Personalization: From Mass Customization to the Mass Personalization

Mass customization is the standard production but customers wants to add some features to the standard product (Hu, 2013). For example cars. The consumers can add so many features to their new cars while ordering it, and they are ready to pay more.

Mass production transforms to the new type of production logic: customization and mass customization over the time. Because people wants to differ himself/herself from the others. Today people are talking about personalization and mass personalization.

Personalization is to achieve satisfying each customer as an individual by uncovering their latent needs (Tseng, et al., 2010). In mass customization, production is realized for only customers that are in the niche market.

With flexibility in production and variety in product, modular production capability, mass personalization term is emerged in 1980s. Personalization lets business adapt differentiation strategy and products and services personalized and hence they have added a value instead of competing prices. Ultra personalized product are also an example of focusing benefit (Torn & Vaneker, 2019). Enterprises are accept the extra cost of personalization as its capability to differentiate them from others in the market.

After I 4.0, the new production strategy emerged personalization. Personalization in reality is very similar with the craft mentality in I1.0. In the Industrial revolution we are live in is like the flash back of I1.0: craft type production. In craft type, production is also a personalized production in that period. Customers are in the production processes from the beginning: design.

There are some differences between mass customization, personalization and mass personalization. In personalization, customers are in the production process from the beginning of the processes: design. Thus, the finished product is completely different after the manufacturing processes (Hu, 2013). In customization, there is standard product and configuration depending on customers. However, in personalization the customer adaptation to the product and production processes are accepted from the beginning to the end of the processes (Tseng et al., 2010). For example when you go to a restaurant you can order a standard meal from the menu and a you will choose specific sauce depending on your taste. This is one example to a customization from a Daily life. On the other hand, when you design a bag and choose the raw materials, accessories for production it is the one basic example for a personalization. Because the product is completely different from the others. You design; you choose the materials and accessories depending on your cultural and design background. The product is only for you: personalized one.

The difference between customization and personalization is summarized in Table 5.

Table 5. The differences between Customization and Personalization

Variables	Customization	Personalization
Customer needs	Known	Some of them are known and other are latent
Physical domain	Product families	Personalization value chain
Process domain	Reconfigurable manufacturing systems	Changeable, adaptable and reconfigurable service processes
Logistic domain	Reconfigurable supply chain networks	Changeable, adaptable and reconfigurable delivery networks

Adapted from Tseng et al., 2010

Since it can be understood from the bag and meal examples, the customer needs are known in the customization. However, in personalization the customers' inherent needs and expectations can be discovered by the help of mathematical algorithms, artificial intelligence etc. another differences showed in Table 5 is physical domain. In the first approach, physical domain is there is some group of products, product families, and production is done according to those product families. On the other hand, in the second approach in personalization, every step in the processes are new and every contribution is benefit for the value chain. In customization processes are reconfigurable depending the product families but in the personalization since there is a new product may in each production period processes can be changed and reconfigurable totally depending on the product type. There is a point on the table x that should be explained in processes domain of the personalization is explained as "service processes". It is because of the the most of the expectations of customers are not known in the beginning of the processes and also customers are also the maker as a part of the manufacturing processes from the design processes it is explained as "service processes. Because the processes becomes service processes, more than a manufacturing processes. Also logistic processes are used the same manner with the processes domain.

Since every object, every machine and every device are digitalized with the help of IoT, connected and communicate each other from end to end, from suppliers to the customers with the help of high-speed internet, requesting the customer needs and supplying them is become easier than before (Castaño et al, 2019). It is why the personalization and personalized production is more possible than ever thus, customers can produce the product that they design it with the help of producers that have the proper resources to do it. This consumer/prosumer- producer contact and collaboration facilitate to understand customers' expectations and make design processes easily by the help of customers. Enormously increasing in collaboration among robot-human-machine and with the help of artificial intelligence in I5.0, it is easier to do manufacture personalized product than before.

As the main theme of I5.0, personalization firstly focuses on customer and tries to understand their expectations. after mass customization people wants to differentiate the products they are using and also wants to Express themselves via designing and being the parts of a production. Especially it appears as a fashion in shoe, clothes, bag, accessories etc. as the preferences and necessity (medical care, medical drugs etc.) of the people. In addition, people wants to differentiate themselves and product they are using the social group that are being in (Oliveira, Cunha & Carvalho, 2019). Customers' expectations is the focus of personalization.

The number of enterprises works with customers in any stage of the production process is enormously increasing today. The reason for that is enterprises are try to adherence to the principle of increasing customer satisfaction as to involve them to the processes from the designing, prototyping, manufacturing and feedback. In order to decide the right product the customers should involve to the processes from the beginning. Consumer is works with producer and he/she becomes a consumer + producer let us say: prosumer (Shang et al., 2019). Thus, people does not pay too much to Express themselves and their ideas, show their creativity and produce want they design and want.

Characteristics of I5.0 such as flexible production, collaborative robots, form end-to-end communication, communication between customers and producer via online channel, making decision instantly, and robots with artificial intelligence facilitate to adapt personalization principle.

Personalized manufacturing is costly in case of mold/models, machines, materials and tools should be changed for each product type. In addition, designing and art works are higher the costs and directly to the prices. However, in mass personalization those cost handicaps try to surpass and costs decreases. Started from the I4.0 working without man, light, climate is also the main cost decreasing elements of I.5.0. Besides, artificial intelligence decrease the managerial and White color workers costs. Thus, mass personalization costs decreased properly.

3.2. Sharing Economy and GIG Economy

Firstly began in real estate (for example: Airbnb) and transportation (for example: Uber) sector sharing economy is aimed to use idle resources and regain them to the economy (Stemler, 2016). The unused houses are hire/rent. In addition, vehicles are uses inside outside of the city for the sake of gaining money.

Gig economy has direct relations with the sharing economy. Gig economy (job for a once) is doing job wherever you want to do from even from your home, whenever you want to do and for how long and how many times even for a once to do. This mentality is also emerged designing and producing whatever you want do produce/make idea (Woodcock & Graham, 2019: 10). In sharing economy, idle resources are being used and in gig economy, the logic is same. There is a designer or any person without any knowledge about the processes but have willing to do and pay the price of it lets say gig worker, and there are idle resources such as machines, robots, devices, building and may be capital whatever related to make the production real.

Key features of gig work is summarized in the followings (Stewart and Stanford, 2017; Burtch, Carnahan & Greenwood, 2018; Hall & Krueger, 2018):

- Gig works has irregular and their own schedule depending on demands
- Gig workers has to have the equipment's to perform the job
- In some of the cases the gig works has to have the workplace to do the jobs
- Gig jobs and gig workers are organized via digital platforms, web services (digital intermediary).

Gig working platforms (digital platforms) facilitates and mediates relationship between workers supply and and consumer/professional demand and for finishing a small tasks (gig works) (Attia, Aziz, Friedman & Elhusseiny, 2011). There is no managerial directions and rules and no hierarchy between groups. According to Gandini (2019) the most important and interesting aspects of Gig works are given below:

- There is no specific designated workplace for gig works.
- Since there is no workplace there is no managerial directions

- Managerial controls just is on the performance of gig workers by means of feedback, rating and ranking systems via platform (especially digital based) they are within and by monitoring data the system has been collected.

There are so many examples and platforms to match the gig works and gig workers together for micro tasks or gigs. The main platform based working examples are homerun.com, armut.com. taskrabbit.com., Freelancer.com, Upwork.com, etc. for example in armut.com. you can hire a person for a different task such as; home cleaning, plumber, house painting and exterior printing (homerun.com; armut.com, 01.02.2021). Work furniture assembly, Tv mounting, handyman, snow removing, help moving, delivery service, winter tasks, virtual- online tasks etc. are some of the services Taskrabbit can give at once (TasRabbit.com, 01.02.2021). Gig workers are selected by consumers by the ratings and performance from their old jobs. Those click based works are the main examples for digital platforms matches consumer and producer, freelancer etc.

3.3. Crowdsourcing

Social media, internet and mobile technologies facilitate to make decision by crowd homogenously and quickly from appropriate platforms. To take advice and ask to the crowd with the help of social networks and outsource their resources are crowdsourcing (Brabham, 2013: 3).

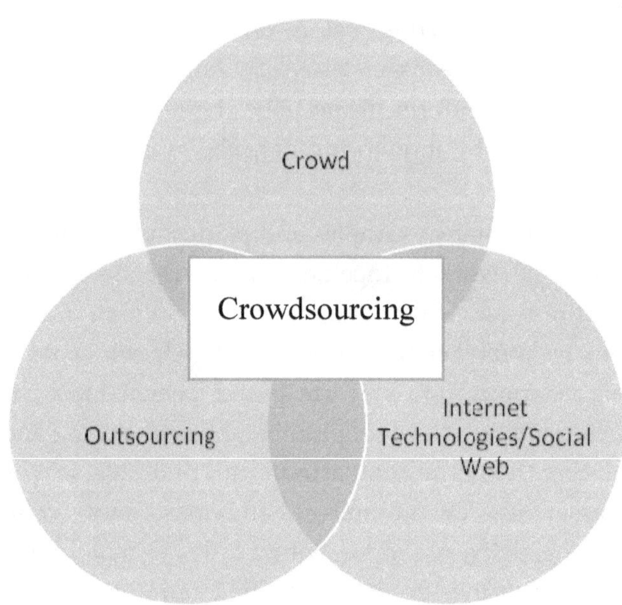

Figure 15. The relations between outsourcing, crowd, and internet technologies

As shown in Figure 15 it is clear that the crowdsourcing is doing the job by means of the group of people and power&sinergy of crowd according to the principle of outsourcing via social web and internet. Rather than opens, the job by only Professional in outsourcing in crowdsourcing the job is opens to everyone. Another difference in crowdsourcing from an traditional way of doing job is any job is done by the help of a group of professional or non-professional who are willing to and using the related social-digital platform in which the group of people meet for the same goals. So crowdsourcing also explained by scholars as" an online distributed problem solving and production model in which connected people collaborate for a specific task" (Vukovic, 2009). According to the scholars Hammon and Hippner (2012) the chances of crowdsourcing are in the followings:

- The system allows to Access and share knowledge and data on digital platforms
- Ability to establish and mediate relationships between enterprise and customers
- Increase of brand loyalty
- Ability to understand and discover of consumers' needs
- Better solutions for problems
- Modularity and flexibility on processes
- Highly modular and flexible processes and less time-to-market
- Decrease in processes and whole costs

Crowdsourcing is very powerful tool to take advice and get ideas of crowds via social platforms with the help of online from your mobile devices. This method is useful tool for designing new product, developing a product and solving specific problems without paying anything. People shared their ideas are not always professionals besides; the most of them are non-professional.

Sometimes crowdsourcing is confused with e-business, e-trade. The processes are same in using web technologies but crowdsourcing change the web platforms to collaborative social production platforms and the consumers becomes to the content creators (Saxton et al., 2013).

According to Vukovic (2009) the four stage of crowdsourcing process are: registration and specification, initialize crowdsourcing contest, carry our crowdsourcing request, and complete crowdsourcing request. In the registration and specification of the stage providers and requestors registers the platform. In the second stage the platform, announce the crowdsourcing request as an open call. In the third and last stages platform acts as broker between requester and broker in establishing IP governance and after completion the task submission and validations are the following sub processes.

Amazon's Mechanical Turk is one of the example of crowdsourcing. In this platform, businesses and individuals can perform their tasks virtually (Amazon Mechanical Turk, (www.mturk.com). They defined jobs as micro tasks because even a big Project can be divided as its work packages and some virtually by so many different groups in a global perspective by the help of crowdsourcing principles.

<table>
<tr><td>

Tips
Amazon Mechanical Turk
Amazon Mechanical Turk is the crowdsourcing Marketplace for individuals and businesses to a digitally connected people who are willing to do the job virtually. According to Howe (2006), Amazon took the Turk name after the chess machine created by mathematician Wolfgang von Kempelen. It is kind of an automated chessboard.

Howe, 2006
</td></tr>
</table>

Social media platform usage like in crowdsourcing makes paradigm changes in production: Social Manufacturing.

3.4. Social Manufacturing

After personalization, the new production mentality is the Social Manufacturing. Social manufacturing is to combine the producer and consumer in a one platform. Today enterprises are working prosumer as a new type of producer/consumer within a harmony.

Spreading logic of cyber physical system with the help of industrial internet via some of the social networks (Facebook, LinkedIn etc.) Professional and nonprofessionals make a contact with enterprises to take a part of designing, production, logistic etc. as producer, marketer, and consumer. In order to help also nonprofessionals enterprises are opened their resources for everyone. Social manufacturing logic increases the social resource usage, enterprises are becoming the society centered self-managing organizations, CPS are becoming Cyber Physical Social Systems (CPSSs) and social media communication is enormously increasing (Jiang et al., 2016). Thus, production ecosystem is becoming social manufacturing environment that everybody is communicate each other and development in every stage is possible.

Social manufacturing mentality helps to create a team synergy as facilitate to gather Professional and nonprofessionals from the beginning of the processes. This production environment is specifically customer-oriented environment and facilitate to transform personalized production ecosystem (Shang et al., 2019). With the help of social manufacturing every participant of the production processes has added a value to the value chain and every customers has ability to involve the processes in each stage thus enterprises will gain a better position in the competitive market they are in.

In Social manufacturing understanding people that are not related to the production stages and designing as a hobby and produce it with 3D printers becomes maker.

In a summary social manufacturing understanding (Jiang et al., 2016):

- Prosumer is the main actor of the production
- CPSs are transforms to the CPSSs
- There could be a social communication and interaction between producer and consumer
- Prosumer will be in every stage of the production
- There build an organic network between every participant and the synergy is created.

4. BLOCKCHAIN TECHNOLOGY, CRYPTO CURRENCIES AND CASHLESS SOCIETY

Increasingly wide spreading in digitalization, social manufacturing and IoT the problem will arise with them as well: Security. Verifying data with the help of more than one verifying processes in order to do the jobs in a secure and transparent way for designer, producer, entrepreneur that comes together in virtual platforms without seeing each other physically, is become important subject than ever.

Block chain is the technology that everybody in the processes able to see each other transparently and passing from one stage to other is saved by special passwords (Michael, Cohn and Butcher, 2018). Data transfers from one-step to the other transparently means that everybody in the system can monitor it easily with password. Data are recorded to blocks created by the system. While recording data to the blocks cryptography.

In block, chain there is decentralized peer-to-peer (P2P) network structure. It means that every participant in the system accepted as a peer. They can communicate each other and share data, documents etc. among each other and they do not need a centralized authority. Thus, the time of process and also after I4.0 also in I5.0 this decentralized structure takes a catalyzer roles in making quick and autonomous decision and communication among devices, machines and robots in the CPS.

Every transaction is recorded in order to be serviced every participants transparently. Hence, the security and reliability on finance, design patent etc. subjects is cleared off. The main important and strength parts of system block chain is everybody in the system is passes from the security scanning.

In applications, block chain thought, as the system that facilitate cryptocurrency transactions and it is mainly misused. It is because of crypto currency and finance system is the first that used block chain technology.

Crypto currencies are here to facilitate to make any transaction digitally. Transactions are realized in a very short period in time sometimes in seconds and within very little costs.

5. AFTER COVID-19: THE NEW NORMAL

In the new normal, let us say post-pandemic period enterprises give more importance to digitalization than before the Covid-19 pandemic. They will spend more financial resources on automation and digitalization. By this way, the digitalization process of I4.0 and I5.0 will be completed properly.

The investment on automation and digitalization is of course increase the productivity and efficiency by means of using machines, robots. According to findings of search of The Centre for Economics and Business Research the gross domestic products is increased percentage10 between 1993-2016 because of investing robots (Wilson, ifr.org. 10.01.2021).

Scholars summarized the structure/situation of enterprises in three periods: respond, recover and renew (Garther, 2020).

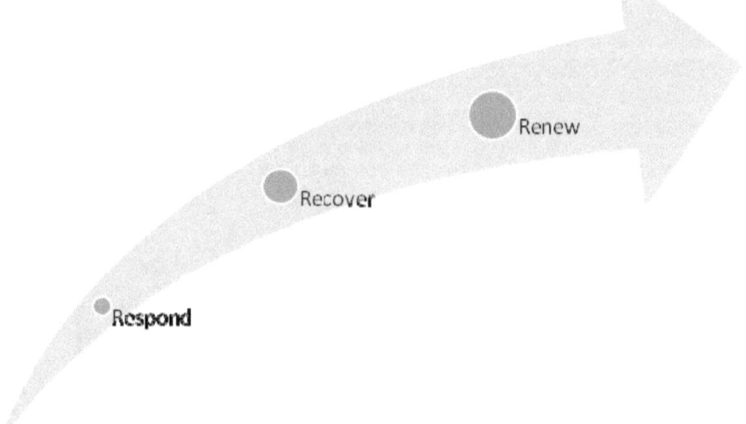

Figure 16. The structure of enterprises in Corono-19 Pandemic and
new normal-post pandemic

Garther, 2020

As summarized in Figure 16 the situation of enterprises with surviving Corona classified into three periods as: Respond, recover and renew. In respond, period people in the enterprises as a completely organizational structure try to understand the pandemic and result of pandemic. The organization try to measure the result and effect of the pandemic on workers, and enterprises, their markets. They try to solve this chaotic situation as possible as they can. They use so many problem understanding and solving technique as brainstorms to make a plan to survive despite the fact that Covid-19 virus environment. This stage can be explained as case study it is the most chaotic and short period.

In the second stage enterprises are try to make a short term plans for recovering and get rid of the result of virus. For example, in tourism determination and realizing the distance precautions and disinfection rules and standards are the main recovering and the style of doing jobs despite the virus. Hospitals have also some precautions in the recovering stage. The establishment of new hospitals and new department in the current hospitals for the Covid-19 positive patients. This stage is action stage so it takes longer than the first period.

The last stage is renewing stage. In this stage, enterprises make strategic plans and take precautions in order to stop the spreading effect of virus. This stage is also the speeding up the digitalization and automation process. Especially in physical touching point's digitalization and automation process in more important than other parts. In these points, man gives its roles to machines& robots. At these points kiosks, computers, robots, sensors and other devices and computer assistance will do the rest of the work instead of human. The new business models are coming for this stage.

6. REAL LIFE CASES

There are so many examples about I5.0, I40, CPS, IoT, Co-Bots etc. In this part of the book, the selected real case examples and applications will be given in order to give a vision to the readers.

- **Flipped classrooms**: It is the implication of Industry 4.0 and 5.0 principle to the education. In this type of education model, the conventional education is redesigned as digital World and new generation learning expectations. As a Blended Learning (BL), model Flipped classrooms facility to reaching and learning from the online context (videos, articles, journals, podcasts etc.). After reaching and learning from digital materials students able to ask and learn further from the teacher in the classes (Herman, Dareng and Bakri 2020).

- **Robots for Education**: VTRAC has widespread of robots also customized for educational purposes. Their educational robots can help students for basic STEM (Science Technology Education Mathematics) functions. It has also real time analytics tools to monitor students' progress (https://www.vtracrobotics.com/portfolio/education/, 17.01.2021).

- **Autonomous Cars:** this type of cars does not need any pilot and can drive by themselves. In addition, there is also an opportunity not to owing and paying a car but it is possible to hire a car like a registering the system like Uber etc. Companies like Uber own their cars in fleet and send it directly to the customer who need them without any driver in it (Kane, 2016, MIT Sloan Management Review, 01.01.2021). Driverless option is not limited with cars there is as application of public buses. In Malaga/Spain, there is an attempt to use buses with electric without driver control (Fleming, 2021, World Economic Forum).

- **Emergency management:** as an application of IoT, researchers construct a fire alarming system in order to raise the nations firefighting management and emergency management level (Ji & Anwen, 2010). Also in chemical industry, scholars use the CPS to provide an urgent information on critical processes and items (Squire &Song, 2014). Another example is from Dublin and it is about preventing theft on water safety ring buoys (Wray, 2021, Cities-Today.com).

- **Smart Traffic**: There are so many smart traffic applications such as collecting and monitoring real time information and control the traffic flow to prevent traffic congestions (Cao, Li and Zhang, 2011); automatic identification of vehicles (Xiao &Wang, 2011), Smart poles in Seoul acting as streetlight, traffic light, environment sensors, footfall counter, smartphone charges, Wi-Fi Access point, Close Circuit Television (CCTV) (Wray, cities-to-day.com17.03.2021).

- **Smart cities**: one of the applications of I5.0 technologies in Lisbon is by using sensors to gathering real time data about city pollution, noise, weather temperature, wind, traffic etc. (https://smartcity.brussels/news-598-smart-city-lisbon, 01.05.2020).

- **Smart helmets and wearable devices**: there is an increasing trend in wearable devices in this new era. In China Polices, wear smart helmets to detecting people with high fewer with in a distance of 5-meter radius (CNBC, 21.01.2021).

- **Smart hospitals**: Hospitals will be equipped with smart flexible wearable embedded with RFID tags which will be give into the patients on arrivals, through which not just doctors but nurses will also be able to monitor heart rate, blood pressure, temperature and other conditions of patients inside or outside the premises of hospital (Fuhrer & Guinard, 2006)

- **Smart hotels:** Wynn hotel in Las Vegas has announced in December 2016 that it will introduce in all its rooms Amazon's Echovoice-controlledspeaker, equipped with the Alexa digital assistant (Amazon, 01.02.2021), while Aloft Hotels use Siri (USA Today, 2016).

  In 2014 Aloft Hotels started testing a delivery robot developed by Savioke (Savioke, 2021). This robot can navigate the hotel, use the elevator, and call the guest room to deliver requested items to the customer's doorstep.

  In 2016, Hilton hotels launched a robotic concierge "Connie" that is powered by artificial intelligence. Also no need to mention about Henn- Na Hotel in Japan! (https://www.h-n-h.jp/en/facilities)

- **Humanoid robots-** Brian: Brian is the name of human robots for elder's healthcare. It is social and interactive humanoid robots. It can express its basic feelings. It can be happy, sad and show its mimics (Louie, McColl, & Nejat, 2014).

- **A Robot Waiter in a Restaurant**: Pizza Hut has recruited humanoid robot Pepper to take customer orders in a conversational manner. Pepper uses voice recognition and artificial intelligence to communicate with customers. It is also equipped with a special app developed by Pizza Hut (https://futurism.com/meet-pepper-the-robot-pizza-huts-newest-crew-member, 11.02.2021).

- **Bellboy robots- Sacarino**: Sacarino is the bellboy in hotels for help customers, give information to them and answer their questions during their stay in hotel (López, Pérez, Zalama, & Gómez-García-Bermejo, 2013).

- **Wearable devices**: some wearable devices and clothes a detect your health problems and solve them. For example SomnaPatch can detect your sleep apnea and measures; pulse rate, nasal pressure, blood oxygen, etc. (Barack, 2017, Gear Brain). There are also wearable devices for diabetics to monitor glucose levels (USA Today, 16.02.2021). Some wearables are monitor hearth rhythm, EKG (Alivecor.com, 15.01.2021).

- **VR in Recreational Facilities (Museums):** there is a widespread usage of VR/AR technologies in museums. For example, in The Städel Museums you have a chance to have an experience with travelling 200 years ago via VR apps (The Städel Museum, 01.03.2020).

SCENARIOS FOR SERVICE INDUSTRIES

7. SCENARIOS FOR SERVICE INDUSTRIES

The major components of I 5.0 ecosystem are objects/things. The physical objects should be integrated to the cyber system by means of sensors, actuators etc. Thus, the monitoring of physical things are more easy and efficient which are connected to the cyber world after all.

The enterprises should firstly started to digitalize their physical objects and make them connected among each other appropriately. The main question that should be answered is which are the objects/products that have to be enter in the beginning to the cyber space. There is no one answer for this question. The answers depends on the sectors is being in, the type and attribute of the product and the mainly depends on the conditions which are now the enterprises being in: Covid-19!

Enterprises are now faced with the big problem and they try to recover from this pandemic. In the first implementation, it is possible to decrease the level of physical contact the personnel. In order to facilitate the implementation the main scenario approach is held for Check-In (C/I) and Checkout (C/O) process.

Although I4.0 and I5.0 implementation started in the manufacturing industries, it is infant and intangible for service industries. Scenario based approach makes it more understandable and tangible of subject the I5.0 for service industries (Weidenhaupt, Pohl, Jarke, & Haumer, 1998). Scenarios represents examples for how to systems works and leads. Thus, a scenario is one possible behavior limited to a set of purposeful interactions taking place among several agents (Achour, 1998). Besides, in scenario based approaches scenarios and structured definitions of real world problems by means of support active learning (Erol, Jäger, Hold, Ott, & Sihn, 2016).

Scenario based approaches helps to have a vision how to solve current real world problems and how the technology improve the current processes (Nardi, 1992). Thus, scenario based approach facilitate to understand the implication of I5.0 principles for service industries.

7.1. Check-In and Check Out Processes

In this part, we will make our scenarios for two main processes that exist in most of the service industries. They are Check In (C/I) and Check Out (C/O).

The Covid-19 restrictions and shutdowns affected the hospitality industry more than any other sector. According to The World Tourism Organization (UNWTO) the arrivals in 2020 march has dropped 60 percent comparing to the last year 2019. Also inbound and outbound tourism expenditures are declined between 55 and 68 percent globally around the world. (https://unstats.un.org, 21.01.2021). Therefore, if the sector has managed to work without physical contact with customers they will survive under this devastating economic conditions. As far as they realized the digital transformation, is concerned how could it be?

There are some real world examples for digital transformation like hotel staffed with robots (Henna Hotel, 2020; Hilton Hotel, 2020), drones based delivery service (Amazon, 2020).

There is also no doubt to say the most crucial sector is the health in these catastrophic times. There are some attempts for digital transformation of hospitals like; fog computing technology to gather the data from telemedicine system (Kumari, Tanwar, Tyagi, & Kumar, 2018), representing the general framework for patient centered hospital models(Afferni, Merone, & Soda, 2018), using holograms additive manufacturing, VR principles in hospitals (Merril, Notaroberto, Laby, Rabinowitz, & Piemme, 1992; Schultheis & Rizzo, 2001).

In this part of the book scenario based approach is utilized for arrival, departure operations for service enterprises. Arrival and departure processes terms defined such as:

- Arrival Process-Check-In (C/I): the terms stand for arrivals for any service industries. Those arrivals and demands can be physically and online. Some of the examples are; reservations to a hotel, registration to a hospital and give and order in a restaurant.

- Departure Process Check-Out (C/O): C/O means the last processes one should do before leaving from the enterprise. Some of the examples are an ordinary C/O for hotels, patient discharge like payment and showing test results to the MD and payment in a restaurant.

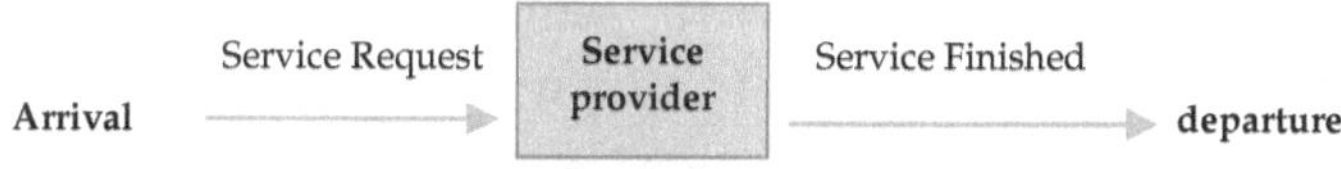

Figure 17. Arrivals and Departures

7.1.1. Approach

Operations in an enterprises starts with customer's arrivals and demanding a service. Those arrivals can be defined as arrivals (hotel, supermarkets, etc.) request (for example in consulting agency) and orders (For example in a restaurant). Besides, physically those arrivals could be also online. In this part of the book, scenarios will be created for the implications of I5.0 in arrivals and departures processes. In other words, scenarios will be created for the entrance to the Front Office (FO) and departures from the Back Office (BO) borders. Multi- scenarios will be created for those processes. Figure 18 represent the general framework of the approach.

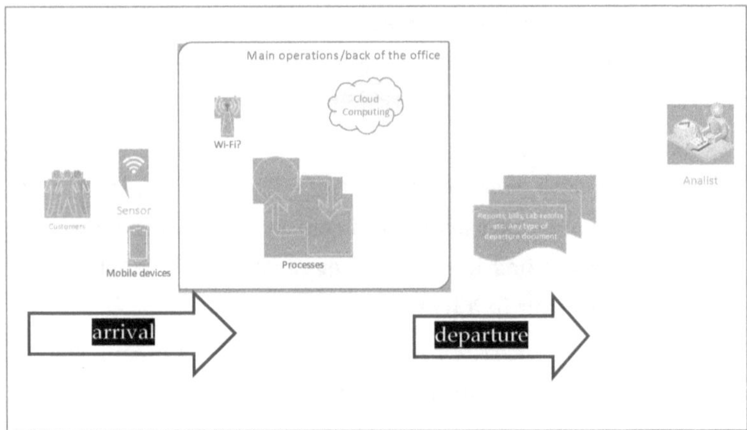

Figure 18. General framework for the system

Figure 18 shows the general framework of the system proposed in this study. The system inputs are the main demands/request of customers. Demands/request of customers can be reached to the enterprise via any type of online channel without going to the enterprise or customers can be shown physically in the system.

Table 6. Scenarios for arrival operations

Arrival to the service point :arrival type can be physically or virtually (via online devices/channels)
Multiple scenarios: • Type 1 Arrivals': customers know the enterprise and its services. They know which type of service they want to demand, they are aware of the services. In this case, the standard procedure can be applied about the services. • Type 2 Arrivals: customers do not have any idea about the services given and what help. In this case, interaction level should be high and any type of interactive devices should be integrated.
Example from service industry: hospitals labs registration, hotel C/I, restaurants ordering
Possible Industry 5.0 solution: • Mobile devices or any type of electronic devices contacted to the internet (kiosks, tablets etc.), sensors especially elderly people and handicaps. • Robots for detailed explanation (equipped with AI wherever possible), any type of mobile devices.

In Table 6, we have two types of arrivals and two solutions for both of them. In the first case, consumers know the service and may be have an experience. In this case, basic types of technological solutions solve the consumer's problems and help them.

In the second case, arrivals do not have an idea about the service given by the enterprises. In this case, interaction level should be higher. In order to use I5.0 technologies it is suggested to use robots donated with AI.

Table 7. Scenarios for departure operations

Departure from the service point: departure type can be physically or virtually in case of transaction held via online)
Scenario: customers leave the enterprise after being served. In this case, they make the payment and have their invoices.
Example from service industry: hospitals labs result, hotel C/O, restaurant payment
Possible Industry 5.0 solution: robots, mobile devices, sensors.

In departure, customer leaves the enterprise after closing the outstanding amount. In hospitals after payment and whole, the processes the patient should have the laboratory result or doctor report. Another example is in hotels before leaving you can have invoice or any kind of document related with the payment. Hence, in any case robots or any mobile devices can help the customers.

Scenarios explained in the above can help the professionals in the service points in which interaction level is high. Industry 5.0 technologies are expensive since they are new and few. Thus, the starting point can be equipped and implemented I5.0 technologies at the high level of interaction service point.

EPILOGUE

8. DISCUSSION

The most prominent concept that we come across at I4.0 and I5.0 is individualization of products. How the enterprises meet such a huge volume of demand at individualization at its peak period. Do they hold on to hundreds of designs, molds, and models? Alternatively, the time we live in, the COVID-19 era will eventually lead people to consume less, save more. Will this result in instead of having many watches, furniture has or shoes people have only one that is unique for themselves. Thus, would this lead to less production but more of a time devoted for individualized product, and would result in diminishing production volumes? All of these needs to be questioned. The modern understanding of "band vagon" mentality seems to leave its place to more sensible production patterns. The most likely is that near future will dictate its mandate to all of us.

The time and conditions we are living in showed us we need touchless work and less workers. The human resource (HR) mentality is transformed to a different pace. HR needs person:

- have ability to work on a different software languages
- Keen to work in a distanced space/place?
- Can work in a more than one teams and social groups at once
- Can do more than one job in a same working period
- Can use mobile technology properly
- Able to analyze big data and see the latent pattern in it
- Find a solution to a problem and make a decision very quickly
- Keen to robots& AI Technologies
- Can work in a flexible conditions

In Post Covid, in the new era the human resource is also faced with paradigm change.

CLOSING REMARKS

Is the pandemic has an effect on people to behave more economical and do the most of the jobs for himself/herself? Is this facilitate on personalization and doing him/her own product, designs which comes with I5.0. Is it possible work with robots as designing your own product? Will the production lines replaced with the lean factories, less products and services in means of amounts and variety? Do the enterprises and people be more sensitive in case of sustainability and using natural resources? Will we be alone and isolated from the society at last?

Instead of eating our meals, do we drink only our supplements instead of eating? May be we will prepare our own meals with 3D,4D or 5D printers like astronaut?

Do the AI or human brain win? Do the AI who wins the Kasparov, take the managerial positions or already did? Who make decision Man or Machine?

REFERENCES

Achour, C. B. (1998, May). Guiding Scenario Authoring. In *EJC* : 152-171

Additively. (2020). Why ideas fail and how AM can help.

AIBO. (2020). Aibo's trick. Retrieved from https://us.aibo.com/contents/

Aktımur, B., & Gökpinar, E. (2015). Katmanlı Üretimin Havacılıkdaki Uygulamaları. *Gazi Üniversitesi Fen Bilimleri Dergisi Part: C, Tasarım Ve Teknoloji*, 463-469.

Alcisto, J., Enriquez, A., Garcia, H., Hinkson, S., Steelman, T., Silverman, E., ... Es-Said, O. S. (2011). Tensile Properties and Microstructures of Laser-Formed Ti-6Al-4V. *Journal of Materials Engineering and Performance, 20*(2), 203-212. doi:10.1007/s11665-010-9670-9

Alkhamisi, A. O., Arabia, S., & Monowar, M. M. (2013). Rise of augmented reality: Current and future application areas. *International journal of internet and distributed systems, 1*(04), 25.

Alpaydin, E. (2020). *Introduction to machine learning*: MIT press.

Appelbaum, S. H. (1997). Socio ‐ technical systems theory: an intervention strategy for organizational development. *Management decision.*

Asif, M., Lee, J. H., Lin-Yip, M. J., Chiang, S., Levaslot, A., Giffney, T., ... Aw, K. C. (2018). A new photopolymer extrusion 5-axis 3D printer. *Additive Manufacturing, 23*, 355-361.

Asimo, https://honda.com.tr/asimo, 9.08.2020.

Attia, A. M., Aziz, N., Friedman, B., & Elhusseiny, M. F. (2011). Commentary: The impact of social networking tools on political change in Egypt's "Revolution 2.0". *Electronic commerce research and applications, 10*(4), 369-374.

Azuma, R., Baillot, Y., Behringer, R., Feiner, S., Julier, S., & MacIntyre, B. (2001). Recent advances in augmented reality. *IEEE computer graphics and applications, 21*(6), 34-47.

Azuma, R. T. (1997). A Survey of Augmented Reality. *Presence: Teleoperators and Virtual Environments,* 6(4), 355-385. doi:10.1162/pres.1997.6.4.355

Azuma, R. T. (2016). The most important challenge facing augmented reality. *Presence: Teleoperators and Virtual Environments, 25*(3), 234-238.

Bae, H., Golparvar-Fard, M., & White, J. (2013). High-precision vision-based mobile augmented reality system for context-aware architectural, engineering, construction and facility management (AEC/FM) applications. *Visualization in Engineering, 1*(1), 1-13.

Barack, L. (2017). SomnaPatch wearable knows if you are breathing—or not. Gear Brain, https://www.gearbrain.com/sleep-wearable-detects-your-breathing-2432895837.html

Beigl, M., & Gellersen, H. (2003). *Smart-its: An embedded platform for smart objects.* Paper presented at the Smart Objects Conference (sOc).

Billinghurst, M., & Kato, H. (1999). *Collaborative mixed reality.* Paper presented at the Proceedings of the First International Symposium on Mixed Reality.

Bimber, O., & Raskar, R. (2005). *Spatial augmented reality: merging real and virtual worlds*: CRC press.

Boboc, R. G., Horaţiu, M., & Talabă, D. (2014). An educational humanoid laboratory tour guide robot. *Procedia-Social and Behavioral Sciences, 141,* 424-430.

Boyes, H., Hallaq, B., Cunningham, J., & Watson, T. (2018). The industrial internet of things (IIoT): An analysis framework. *Computers in industry, 101,* 1-12.

Brabham, D. C. (2013). *Crowdsourcing.* Mit Press.

Braun, D. H., & Inhofer, S. (2014). Bionic Skin–Disartificialising architecture. *GBT-Institute for Building Technology*.

Britannica. (2020 July 13). Virtual reality. Retrieved from https://www.britannica.com/technology/virtual-reality#ref884304

Bugge, M. M., Hansen, T., & Klitkou, A. (2016). What is the bioeconomy? A review of the literature. *Sustainability, 8*(7), 691.

Burgard, W., Cremers, A. B., Fox, D., Hähnel, D., Lakemeyer, G., Schulz, D., ... & Thrun, S. (1998, July). The interactive museum tour-guide robot. In *Aaai/iaai* (pp. 11-18).

Burtch, G., Carnahan, S., & Greenwood, B. N. (2018). Can you gig it? An empirical examination of the gig economy and entrepreneurial activity. *Management Science, 64*(12), 5497-5520.

Campbell, I., Bourell, D., & Gibson, I. (2012). Additive manufacturing: rapid prototyping comes of age. *Rapid Prototyping Journal*.

Cao, Y., Li, W., & Zhang, J. (2011). *Real-time traffic information collecting and monitoring system based on the internet of things.* Paper presented at the 2011 6th International Conference on Pervasive Computing and Applications.

Cardoso, J., Winkler, M., Voigt, K., & Berthold, H. (2009). *IoS-based services, Platform Services, SLA and Models for the Internet of Services.* Paper presented at the International Conference on Software and Data Technologies.

Carmigniani, J., Furht, B., Anisetti, M., Ceravolo, P., Damiani, E., & Ivkovic, M. (2011). Augmented reality technologies, systems and applications. *Multimedia Tools and Applications, 51*(1), 341-377. doi:10.1007/s11042-010-0660-6

Castaño, F., Strzelczak, S., Villalonga, A., Haber, R. E., & Kossakowska, J. (2019). Sensor reliability in cyber-physical systems using internet-of-things data: A review and case study. *Remote sensing, 11*(19), 2252.

Chin, W. H., Fan, Z., & Haines, R. (2014). Emerging technologies and research challenges for 5G wireless networks. *IEEE Wireless Communications, 21*(2), 106-112.

References

Choi, Y. M., Lee, M. G., & Jeon, Y. (2017). Wearable biomechanical energy harvesting technologies. *Energies, 10*(10), 1483.

Crnjac, M., Veža, I., & Banduka, N. (2017). From concept to the introduction of industry 4.0. *International Journal of Idustrial Engineering and Management, 8*, 21.

CSAIL, M. (2020, July 13). Augmented and Virtual Reality. Retrieved from http://groups.csail.mit.edu/hcie/files/classes/engineering-interactive-technologies/2018-fall/10-03-wed-augmented-reality.pdf

Da Xu, L., He, W., & Li, S. (2014). Internet of things in industries: A survey. *IEEE Transactions on industrial informatics, 10*(4), 2233-2243.

Dalkıran, H. P. Holografi Tekniğinin Haritacılık Alanında Uygulanması.

Dawood, N., Marasini, R., & Dean, J. (2008). 19 VR–Roadmap: A vision for 2030 in the built environment. *Virtual Futures for Design, Construction and Procurement*, 261.

Dunston, P. S., & Wang, X. (2011). An iterative methodology for mapping mixed reality technologies to AEC operations. *Journal of Information Technology in Construction (ITcon), 16*(30), 509-528.

Erol, S., Jäger, A., Hold, P., Ott, K., & Sihn, W. (2016). Tangible Industry 4.0: a scenario-based approach to learning for the future of production. *Procedia CiRp, 54*, 13-18.

Esteva, A., Robicquet, A., Ramsundar, B., Kuleshov, V., DePristo, M., Chou, K., ... Dean, J. (2019). A guide to deep learning in healthcare. *Nature medicine, 25*(1), 24-29.

European Economic and Social Committee. (2020). Industry 5.0. Retrieved from https://www.eesc.europa.eu/en/agenda/our-events/events/industry-50, 5.05.2020

Farooq, M. U., Waseem, M., Mazhar, S., Khairi, A., & Kamal, T. (2015). A review on internet of things (IoT). *International Journal of Computer Applications, 113*(1), 1-7.

Feng, Z., Duh, H. B., & Billinghurst, M. (2008, 15-18 Sept. 2008). *Trends in augmented reality tracking, interaction and display: A review of ten years of ISMAR.* Paper presented at the 2008 7th IEEE/ACM International Symposium on Mixed and Augmented Reality.

Frei, F. X. (2006). Breaking the trade-off between efficiency and service. *Harvard business review, 84*(11), 92.

Fuhrer, P., & Guinard, D. (2006). *Building a smart hospital using RFID technologies: use cases and implementation*: Department of Informatics-University of Fribourg Fribourg, Switzerland.

Gandini, A. (2019). Labour process theory and the gig economy. *Human Relations, 72*(6), 1039-1056.

Gartner. (2020, August 10). An Executive's Guide to Returning to the Workplace. Retrieved from https://www.gartner.com/en/insights/framework-for-post-pandemic-planning

Geels, F. W. (2004). From sectoral systems of innovation to socio-technical systems: Insights about dynamics and change from sociology and institutional theory. *Research policy, 33*(6-7), 897-920.

GE Turkey. (2020, July 16). Katmanlı İmalat (GE Additive). Retrieved from https://geturkiyeblog.com/ge-teknolojileri/katmanli-imalat/

Ghuloum, H. (2010). *3D hologram technology in learning environment.* Paper presented at the Informing Science & IT Education Conference.

Grinin, L., & Grinin, A. (2020). The cybernetic revolution and the future of technologies. In *The 21st Century Singularity and Global Futures* (pp. 377-396). Springer, Cham.

Grunwald, A. (2016). Synthetic biology: seeking for orientation in the absence of valid prospective knowledge and of common values. In *The argumentative turn in Policy analysis* (pp. 325-344). Springer, Cham.

Harayama, Y. (2020). Society 5.0: Aiming for a New Human-centered Society

References

Japan's Science and Technology Policies for Addressing Global Social Challenges. Retrieved from https://www.hitachi.com/rev/archive/2017/ r2017_06/pdf/p08-13_TRENDS.pdf

Hall, J. V., & Krueger, A. B. (2018). An analysis of the labor market for Uber's driver-partners in the United States. *Ilr Review, 71*(3), 705-732.

Hammon, L., & Hippner, H. (2012). Crowdsourcing. *Business & Information systems engineering, 4*(3), 163-166.

Harb, A. (2011). Energy harvesting: State-of-the-art. *Renewable Energy, 36*(10), 2641-2654.

Hatcher, W. G., & Yu, W. (2018). A survey of deep learning: Platform

Herman, T., Dareng, S. Y., & Bakri, Z. (2020, April). Education for industry revolution 4.0: using flipped classroom in mathematics learning as alternative. In *Journal of Physics: Conference Series* (Vol. 1521, No. 3, p. 032038). IOP Publishing.

Honda. (2020, July 3). Asimo. Retrieved from https://honda.com.tr/asimo

Hossain, E., & Hasan, M. (2015). 5G cellular: key enabling technologies and research challenges. *IEEE Instrumentation & Measurement Magazine, 18*(3), 11-21.

Howe, J. (2006). The rise of crowdsourcing. *Wired magazine, 14*(6), 1-4.

Huang, S. H., Liu, P., Mokasdar, A., & Hou, L. (2013). Additive manufacturing and its societal impact: a literature review. *The International Journal of Advanced Manufacturing Technology, 67*(5-8), 1191-1203.

Hu, S. J. (2013). Evolving paradigms of manufacturing: From mass production to mass customization and personalization. *Procedia Cirp, 7*, 3-8.

IEEE-Institute of Engineers and Everyone Else. (2020). Robots, your guide to the world of robotics. Retrieved from https://robots.ieee.org/robots/qrio/

IEEE, https://iot.ieee.org/iot-scenarios.html?prp=oc-1cc8f9b7-1a3f-46f3-8cf2-7167045fd2cc, 01.08.2020

IInternational Organization for Standardization. (2020, July 4). ISO 8373:2012(en)

Robots and robotic devices-Vocabulary. Retrieved from https://www.iso.org/obp/ui/#iso:std:iso:8373:ed-2:v1:en:term:2.9

Information, H. (2020). Ivan Sutherland and Bob Sproull Create the First Virtual Reality Head Mounted Display System. Retrieved from http://www.historyofinformation.com/detail.php?id=861

International Federation of Robotics. (2020). Executive Summary World Robotics 2019 Service Robots. Retrieved from https://ifr.org/downloads/press2018/Executive_Summary_WR_Service_Robots_2019.pdf

Internet of Things Türkiye. (2020). Beacon Teknolojisi Nedir?. Retrieved from https://ioturkiye.com/2019/08/beacon-teknolojisi-nedir/

Isaksson, A. J., Harjunkoski, I., & Sand, G. (2018). The impact of digitalization on the future of control and operations. *Computers & Chemical Engineering, 114,* 122-129.

Javaid, M., & Haleem, A. (2020). Critical components of Industry 5.0 towards a successful adoption in the field of manufacturing. *Journal of Industrial Integration and Management.*

Ji, Z., & Anwen, Q. (2010). *The application of internet of things (IOT) in emergency management system in China.* Paper presented at the 2010 IEEE International Conference on Technologies for Homeland Security (HST).

Jiang, P., Leng, J., & Ding, K. (2016, July). Social manufacturing: a survey of the state-of-the-art and future challenges. In *2016 IEEE International Conference on Service Operations and Logistics, and Informatics (SOLI)* (pp. 12-17). IEEE.

Kanda, T., & Ishiguro, H. (2017). *Human-robot interaction in social robotics*: CRC Press.

References

Kang, H. S., Lee, J. Y., Choi, S., Kim, H., Park, J. H., Son, J. Y., ... Do Noh, S. (2016). Smart manufacturing: Past research, present findings, and future directions. *International Journal of Precision Engineering and Manufacturing-Green Technology, 3*(1), 111-128.

Kaufmann, H. (2003). Collaborative augmented reality in education. *Institute of Software Technology and Interactive Systems, Vienna University of Technology.*

Kilinc, D., & Basegmez, N. (2018). *Uygulamalarla Veri Bilimi Makine Ögrenmesi ve Derin Ögrenme*: Abaküs Kitap.

Kim, S., Vyas, R., Bito, J., Niotaki, K., Collado, A., Georgiadis, A., & Tentzeris, M. M. (2014). Ambient RF energy-harvesting technologies for self-sustainable standalone wireless sensor platforms. *Proceedings of the IEEE, 102*(11), 1649-1666.

Knofius, N., Van der Heijden, M. C., & Zijm, W. H. (2016). Selecting parts for additive manufacturing in service logistics. *Journal of manufacturing technology management.*

Kozma, D., Varga, P., & Soós, G. (2019). Supporting digital production, product lifecycle and supply chain management in industry 4.0 by the arrowhead framework–a survey. In *2019 IEEE 17th International Conference on Industrial Informatics (INDIN)* (Vol. 1, pp. 126-131). IEEE.

Krueger, M. (2020). Videoplace.

Kruth, J.-P., Leu, M.-C., & Nakagawa, T. (1998). Progress in additive manufacturing and rapid prototyping. *CIRP Annals-Manufacturing Technology, 47*(2), 525-540.

Kuka. (2020). Hastane 4.0. Retrieved from https://www.kuka.com/tr-tr/bran%C5%9Flar/%C3%A7%C3%B6z%C3%BCm-veri-bankas%C4%B1/2020/03/hastane-4-0_kuka-laboratuvar-robotlar%C4%B1-kan-%C3%B6rneklerini-gruplara-g%C3%B6re-ay%C4%B1r%C4%B1yor

Kumari, A., Tanwar, S., Tyagi, S., & Kumar, N. (2018). Fog computing for Healthcare 4.0 environment: Opportunities and challenges. *Computers & Electrical Engineering, 72*, 1-13.

LeCun, Y., Bengio, Y., & Hinton, G. (2015). Deep learning. *nature, 521*(7553), 436-444.

Leuski, A., Pair, J., Traum, D., McNerney, P. J., Georgiou, P., & Patel, R. (2006). *How to talk to a hologram.* Paper presented at the Proceedings of the 11th international conference on Intelligent user interfaces.

Levitt, T. (1972). Production-line approach to service. *1972, 52*(5), 41-52.

Levy, G. N., Schindel, R., & Kruth, J.-P. (2003). Rapid manufacturing and rapid tooling with layer manufacturing (LM) technologies, state of the art and future perspectives. *CIRP annals, 52*(2), 589-609.

Lewis, M. A., & Brown, A. D. (2012). How different is professional service operations management?. *Journal of Operations Management, 30*(1-2), 1-11.

Li, X., Shang, J., & Wang, Z. (2017). Intelligent materials: a review of applications in 4D printing. *Assembly Automation.*

Lipton, J. I., Cutler, M., Nigl, F., Cohen, D., & Lipson, H. (2015). Additive manufacturing for the food industry. *Trends in food science & technology, 43*(1), 114-123.

Liu, X. L., Wang, W. M., Guo, H., Barenji, A. V., Li, Z., & Huang, G. Q. (2020). Industrial blockchain based framework for product lifecycle management in industry 4.0. *Robotics and computer-integrated manufacturing, 63*, 101897.

Longo, F., Padovano, A., & Umbrello, S. (2020). Value-oriented and ethical technology engineering in Industry 5.0: a human-centric perspective for the design of the Factory of the Future. *Applied Sciences, 10*(12), 4182.

López, J., Pérez, D., Zalama, E., & Gómez-García-Bermejo, J. (2013). Bellbot-a hotel assistant system using mobile robots. *International Journal of Advanced Robotic Systems, 10*(1), 40.

Louie, W.-Y. G., McColl, D., & Nejat, G. (2014). Acceptance and attitudes toward a human-like socially assistive robot by older adults. *Assistive Technology, 26*(3), 140-150.

References

Lydon, B. (2014). Industry 4.0 - Only One-Tenth of Germany's High-Tech Strategy. https://www.automation.com/en-us/articles/2014-1/industry-40-only-one-tenth-of-germanys-high-tech-s. 21.01.2021

Mastrangelo, D., & Team, B. M. U. " The Use of a Three Dimensional Hologram as an Interface Option" A. Introduction.

Melchels, F. P., Domingos, M. A., Klein, T. J., Malda, J., Bartolo, P. J., & Hutmacher, D. W. (2012). Additive manufacturing of tissues and organs. *Progress in Polymer Science, 37*(8), 1079-1104.

Merril, J. R., Notaroberto, N. F., Laby, D. M., Rabinowitz, A. M., & Piemme, T. E. (1992). The Ophthalmic Retrobulbar Injection Simulator (ORIS): an application of virtual reality to medical education. In *Proceedings of the Annual Symposium on Computer Application in Medical Care* (p. 702). American Medical Informatics Association.

Metters, R., & Vargas, V. (2000). A typology of de-coupling strategies in mixed services. *Journal of Operations Management, 18*(6), 663-682.

Michael, J., Cohn, A. L. A. N., & Butcher, J. R. (2018). Blockchain technology. *The Journal, 1*(7).

Moeuf, A., Pellerin, R., Lamouri, S., Tamayo-Giraldo, S., & Barbaray, R. (2018). The industrial management of SMEs in the era of Industry 4.0. *International Journal of Production Research, 56*(3), 1118-1136.

Nahavandi, S. (2019). Industry 5.0—A human-centric solution. *Sustainability, 11*(16), 4371.

Nardi, B. A. (1992). The use of scenarios in design. *ACM SIGCHI Bulletin, 24*(4), 13-14.

National Research Strategy Bioeconomy 2030. http:// biotech2030.ru/wp-content/uploads/docs/int/bioeconomy_2030-_germany.pdf, 21.01.2021.

Nourbakhsh, I. R., Bobenage, J., Grange, S., Lutz, R., Meyer, R., & Soto, A. (1999). An affective mobile robot educator with a full-time job. *Artificial intelligence, 114*(1-2), 95-124.

Oettmeier, K., & Hofmann, E. (2017). Additive manufacturing technology adoption: an empirical analysis of general and supply chain-related determinants. *Journal of Business Economics, 87*(1), 97-124.

Oliveira, N., Cunha, J., & Carvalho, H. (2019). Co-design and Mass Customization in the Portuguese footwear cluster: an exploratory study. *Procedia CIRP, 84*, 923-929.

Ozkeser, B. (2018). Lean innovation approach in Industry 5.0. *The Eurasia Proceedings of Science, Technology, Engineering & Mathematics, 2*, 422-428.

Paschek, D., Mocan, A., & Draghici, A. (2019). *Industry 5.0-The expected impact of next Industrial Revolution*. Paper presented at the Thriving on Future Education, Industry, Business, and Society, Proceedings of the MakeLearn and TIIM International Conference, Piran, Slovenia.

Paschou, T., Adrodegari, F., Rapaccini, M., Saccani, N., & Perona, M. (2018). Towards Service 4.0: A new framework and research priorities. *Procedia CIRP, 73*(1), 148-154.

Pei, E. (2014). 4D Printing: dawn of an emerging technology cycle. *Assembly Automation*.

Piekarski, W., & Thomas, B. (2002). ARQuake: the outdoor augmented reality gaming system. *Commun. ACM, 45*(1), 36–38. doi:10.1145/502269.502291

Posada, J., Toro, C., Barandiaran, I., Oyarzun, D., Stricker, D., de Amicis, R., .. Vallarino, I. (2015). Visual computing as a key enabling technology for industrie 4.0 and industrial internet. *IEEE computer graphics and applications, 35*(2), 26-40.

Quanjin, M., Rejab, M. R. M., Idris, M. S., Kumar, N. M., Abdullah, M. H., & Reddy, G. R. (2020). Recent 3D and 4D intelligent printing technologies: A comparative review and future perspective. *Procedia Computer Science, 167*, 1210-1219.

Qin, J., Liu, Y., & Grosvenor, R. (2016). A categorical framework of manufacturing for industry 4.0 and beyond. *Procedia CIRP, 52*, 173-178.

References

Rada, M. (2020). INDUSTRY 5.0 definition. https://medium.com/@michael.rada/industry-5-0-definition-6a2f9922dc48,

Rao, B. P., Saluia, P., Sharma, N., Mittal, A., & Sharma, S. V. (2012). *Cloud computing for Internet of Things & sensing based applications.* Paper presented at the 2012 Sixth International Conference on Sensing Technology (ICST).

Rao, S. K., & Prasad, R. (2018). Impact of 5G technologies on industry 4.0. *Wireless personal communications, 100*(1), 145-159.

Reznek, M., Harter, P., & Krummel, T. (2002). Virtual reality and simulation: training the future emergency physician. *Academic Emergency Medicine, 9*(1), 78-87.

Sachsenmeier, P. (2016). Industry 5.0—The relevance and implications of bionics and synthetic biology. *Engineering, 2*(2), 225-229.

Sanders, A., Elangeswaran, C., & Wulfsberg, J. P. (2016). Industry 4.0 implies lean manufacturing: Research activities in industry 4.0 function as enablers for lean manufacturing. *Journal of Industrial Engineering and Management (JIEM), 9*(3), 811-833.

Saxton, G. D., Oh, O., & Kishore, R. (2013). Rules of crowdsourcing: Models, issues, and systems of control. *Information Systems Management, 30*(1), 2-20.

Savioke. https://www.savioke.com/blog/2014/8/11/your-robot-butler-has-arrived, 01.03.2020

Schultheis, M. T., & Rizzo, A. A. (2001). The application of virtual reality technology in rehabilitation. *Rehabilitation psychology, 46*(3), 296.

Schütte, G. (2018). What kind of innovation policy does the bioeconomy need?. *New biotechnology, 40*, 82-86.

Service Robots. (2020, July 3). Pizza Hut hires robot waiters. Retrieved from https://www.servicerobots.com/blog/pizza-hut-hires-robot-waiters/

Shafiq, S. I., Sanin, C., Toro, C., & Szczerbicki, E. (2015). Virtual engineering object (VEO): Toward experience-based design and manufacturing for industry 4.0. *Cybernetics and Systems, 46*(1-2), 35-50.

Shamim, S., Cang, S., Yu, H., & Li, Y. (2017). Examining the feasibilities of Industry 4.0 for the hospitality sector with the lens of management practice. *Energies, 10*(4), 499.

Shang, X., Shen, Z., Xiong, G., Wang, F. Y., Liu, S., Nyberg, T. R., ... & Guo, C. (2019). Moving from mass customization to social manufacturing: A footwear industry case study. *International Journal of Computer Integrated Manufacturing, 32*(2), 194-205.

Shiotani, S., Tomonaka, T., Kemmotsu, K., Asano, S., Oonishi, K., & Hiura, R. (2006). World's first full-fledged communication robot" Wakamaru" capable of living with family and supporting persons. *Mitsubishi Juko Giho, 43*(1), 44-45.

Shiroishi, Y., Uchiyama, K., & Suzuki, N. (2019). Better actions for society 5.0: using AI for evidence-based policy making that keeps humans in the loop. *Computer, 52*(11), 73-78.

Squire, R., & Song, H. (2014). Cyber - physical systems opportunities in the chemical industry: A security and emergency management example. *Process Safety Progress, 33*(4), 329-332.

Stark, J. (2015). Product lifecycle management. In *Product lifecycle management (Volume 1)* (pp. 1-29). Springer, Cham.

Stemler, A. (2016). Betwixt and between: Regulating the shared economy. *Fordham Urb. LJ, 43*, 31.

Stewart, A., & Stanford, J. (2017). Regulating work in the gig economy: What are the options?. *The Economic and Labour Relations Review, 28*(3), 420-437.

Şeker, A., Diri, B., & Balık, H. H. (2017). Derin öğrenme yöntemleri ve uygulamaları hakkında bir inceleme. *Gazi Mühendislik Bilimleri Dergisi, 3*(3), 47-64.

Tamura, H., Yamamoto, H., & Katayama, A. (2001). Mixed reality: future dreams seen at the border between real and virtual worlds. *IEEE computer graphics and applications,* 21(6), 64-70. doi:10.1109/38.963462

References

Tan, Y. K., & Panda, S. K. (2010). Review of energy harvesting technologies for sustainable wireless sensor network. *Sustainable wireless sensor networks*, 1-30.

TongKe, F. (2013). Smart agriculture based on cloud computing and IOT. *Journal of Convergence Information Technology, 8*(2), 210-216.

Torn, I. A. R., & Vaneker, T. H. (2019). Mass Personalization with Industry 4.0 by SMEs: A concept for collaborative networks. *Procedia manufacturing, 28,* 135-141.

Trejos, N. (2016). https://www.usatoday.com/story/travel/roadwarriorvoices/2016/08/24/aloft-hotels-debut-voice-activated-rooms/89218504/ 01.02.2021

Trist, E. L. (1981). *The evolution of socio-technical systems* (Vol. 2). Toronto: Ontario Quality of Working Life Centre.

Tseng, M. M., Jiao, R. J., & Wang, C. (2010). Design for mass personalization. *CIRP annals, 59*(1), 175-178.

Türkiye'nin Endüstri 4.0 Platformu. (2020, July 1). Endüstri 4.0 ile Katmanlı Üretim. Retrieved from https://www.endustri40.com/endustri-4-0-ile-katmanli-uretim/

TÜSİAD. (2016). Türkiye'nin Küresel Rekabetçiliği için Bir Gereklilik Olarak Sanayi 4.0 Gelişmekte Olan Ekonomi Perspektifi. Retrieved from http://www.tusiad.org/indir/2016/sanayi-40.pdf

Umpleby, S. A. (2008). A Short History of Cybernetics in the United States: The Origin of Cybernetics. *Österreichische Zeitschrift für Geschichtswissenschaften, 19*(4), 28-40.

Unesco. (2020, August 2). Japan pushing ahead with Society 5.0 to overcome chronic social challenges. Retrieved from https://en.unesco.org/news/japan-pushing-ahead-society-50-overcome-chronic-social-challenges

Van Dam, K. H., Nikolic, I., & Lukszo, Z. (Eds.). (2012). *Agent-based modelling of socio-technical systems* (Vol. 9). Springer Science & Business Media.

Van Krevelen, D., & Poelman, R. (2010). A survey of augmented reality technologies, applications and limitations. *International journal of virtual reality, 9*(2), 1-20.

Vlahakis, V., Karigiannis, J., Tsotros, M., Gounaris, M., Almeida, L., Stricker, D., . . . Ioannidis, N. (2001). Archeoguide: first results of an augmented reality, mobile computing system in cultural heritage sites. *Virtual Reality, Archeology, and Cultural Heritage, 9*(10.1145), 584993.585015.

Vukovic, M. (2009). Crowdsourcing for enterprises. In *2009 congress on services-I* (pp. 686-692). IEEE.

Wagner, D., & Schmalstieg, D. (2006). *Handheld augmented reality displays.* Paper presented at the IEEE Virtual Reality Conference (VR 2006).

Wang, C.-X., Haider, F., Gao, X., You, X.-H., Yang, Y., Yuan, D., ... Hepsaydir, E. (2014). Cellular architecture and key technologies for 5G wireless communication networks. *IEEE Communications Magazine, 52*(2), 122-130.

Wang, D., Chen, D., Song, B., Guizani, N., Yu, X., & Du, X. (2018). From IoT to 5G I-IoT: The next generation IoT-based intelligent algorithms and 5G technologies. *IEEE Communications Magazine, 56*(10), 114-120.

Weber, W., & Fussenegger, M. (2012). Emerging biomedical applications of synthetic biology. *Nature Reviews Genetics, 13*(1), 21-35.

Webopedia. (2020, June 30). tele-immersion. Retrieved from https://www.webopedia.com/TERM/T/tele-immersion.html

Weidenhaupt, K., Pohl, K., Jarke, M., & Haumer, P. (1998). Scenarios in system development: current practice. *IEEE software, 15*(2), 34-45.

Wiener, N. (1950). Cybernetics. *Bulletin of the American Academy of Arts and Sciences, 3*(7), 2-4.

Williams, J. (2014). Harvard Business Review Internet of Things: Science Fiction or Business Fact (Report and Resources). *Verizon.*

Wilson, M. (2020). How robots help UK manufacturers face the headwinds of Brexit and COVID-19 coronavirus. Retrieved from https://ifr.org/post/ How-robots-help-UK-manufacturers-face-the-headwinds-of-Brexit-and-COVID-19

References

Wirtschaft, D. (2015). Impulse für Wachstum, Beschäftigung und Innovation. *München: PRpetuum GmbH*.

Woodcock, J., & Graham, M. (2019). *The gig economy*. London: Polity Press.

Wu, Q., Li, G. Y., Chen, W., Ng, D. W. K., & Schober, R. (2017). An overview of sustainable green 5G networks. *IEEE Wireless Communications, 24*(4), 72-80.

Xiao, L., & Wang, Z. (2011). Internet of Things: A new application for intelligent traffic monitoring system. *Journal of networks, 6*(6), 887.

Yılmaz, E. (2015). *Oyunlaştırma*. İstanbul: Abaküs.

Yilmaz, T., Abbasi, N. A., & Akan, O. B. (2019). Millimeter-Wave 5G-enabled internet of things. In *5G-Enabled Internet of Things* (pp. 163-181). CRC Press.

Zhou, F., Duh, H. B.-L., & Billinghurst, M. (2008). *Trends in augmented reality tracking, interaction and display: A review of ten years of IS-MAR*. Paper presented at the 2008 7th IEEE/ACM International Symposium on Mixed and Augmented Reality.

Zhou, K., Liu, T., & Zhou, L. (2015). Industry 4.0: Towards future industrial opportunities and challenges. In *2015 12th International conference on fuzzy systems and knowledge discovery (FSKD)* (pp. 2147-2152). IEEE.

Internet

https://www.eesc.europa.eu/en/agenda/our-events/events/industry-50, 25.10.2020

https://aboutmyronkrueger.weebly.com/videoplace.html, 26.01.2020.

Kane, G.C. (2016). Predicting the Future: How to Engage in Really Long-Term Strategic Digital Planning. https://sloanreview.mit.edu/article/predicting-the-future-how-to-engage-in-really-long-term-strategic-digital-planning/ 01.01.2021.

Wray, S. (2021). Seoul's multifunctional smart poles will soon be able to charge drones Retrieved from https://cities-today.com/

seouls-multifunctional-smart-poles-will-soon-be-able-to-charge-drones/, 22.03.2021.

Wray, S. (2021). Dublin pilots IoT and new procurement approach for water safety. https://cities-today.com/dublin-pilots-iot-and-new-procurement-approach-for-water-safety/. 21.01.2021.

https://smartcity.brussels/news-598-smart-city-lisbon, 01.05.2020

https://www.weforum.org/agenda/2021/03/europe-first-autonomous-electric-buses-spain/, 18.03.2021.

https://www.mturk.com/ 01.02.2020

https://futurism.com/meet-pepper-the-robot-pizza-huts-newest-crew-member, 11.02.2021

Connected Places, 21.01.2021

Innovation brief: Post Pandemic Plaes Introduction. https://cp.catapult.org.uk/news/innovation-brief-post-pandemic-places intro-ductlon/21.01.2021.

https://www.usatoday.com/picture-gallery/tech/2019/06/05/6-wearable-devices-manage-diabetes/1275579001/ 16.02.2021

https://store.kardia.com/ 15.01.2021.

https://www.h-n-h.jp/en/facilities

https://www.vtracrobotics.com/portfolio/education/, 17.01.2021.

How COVID-19 is changing the world: a statistical perspective. https://unstats.un.org/unsd/ccsa/documents/covid19-report-ccsa.pdf

UN https://www.un.org/sustainabledevelopment/news/communications-material/, 01.30.2020

The Städel Museum, https://zeitreise.staedelmuseum.de/en/?gclid=-CjwKCAjwr56IBhAvEiwA1fuqGi8Y-3iUJyMTRqO1K5L3IRNQ-RuJMmxYhvuqwJJO5LnRKZaADAzpuKxoCd40QAvD_BwE, 01.03.2020

Jackkdanial, 15.01.2021. AWS_IOT_services.png, Wikimedia.

homerun.com 01.03.2020

References

armut.com 01.02.2021

Mixabest   https://commons.wikimedia.org/wiki/File:KUKA_Indust-
rial_Robots_IR.jpg 17.07.2007.

https://developer.amazon.com/en-US/alexa/alexa-for-hospitality,
01.02.2021

task rabbit.com 03.04.2021

HotelManagement.net, 2016

https://www.cnbc.com/video/2020/06/02/coronavirus-chinese-
tech-firm-develops-helmet-that-detects-fever.html, 01.21.2021.

www.ingramcontent.com/pod-product-compliance
Lightning Source LLC
LaVergne TN
LVHW051546170726
843492LV00006B/1963